God at Work

God at Work

Loving God and Neighbor Through the Book of Exodus

Anthony B. Bradley

RESOURCE *Publications* · Eugene, Oregon

GOD AT WORK
Loving God and Neighbor Through the Book of Exodus

Copyright © 2025 Anthony B. Bradley. All rights reserved. Except for brief quotations in critical publications or reviews, no part of this book may be reproduced in any manner without prior written permission from the publisher. Write: Permissions, Wipf and Stock Publishers, 199 W. 8th Ave., Suite 3, Eugene, OR 97401.

Resource Publications
An Imprint of Wipf and Stock Publishers
199 W. 8th Ave., Suite 3
Eugene, OR 97401

www.wipfandstock.com

PAPERBACK ISBN: 979-8-3852-2522-4
HARDCOVER ISBN: 979-8-3852-2523-1
EBOOK ISBN: 979-8-3852-2524-8
VERSION NUMBER 07/11/25

Scripture quotations taken from The Holy Bible, New International Version®, NIV®. Copyright © 2011 by Biblica, Inc. Used with permission of Zondervan. All rights reserved worldwide. www.zondervan.com.

To Gerard Van Groningen

Contents

Introduction | 1

Exodus 1:1–14 | 24
Exodus 1:15–22 | 29
Exodus 2:1–8 | 35
Exodus 2:11–25 | 41
Exodus 3 | 47
Exodus 4:1–17 | 53
Exodus 4:18–31 | 60
Exodus 5 | 66
Exodus 6:1–27 | 72
Exodus 6:28—7:13 | 81
Exodus 7:13—11:10 | 85
Exodus 12:1–30 | 91
Exodus 12:31–51 | 97
Exodus 13:1–16 | 103
Exodus 13:17—14:31 | 108

Exodus 15:1–21 | 114
Exodus 15:22—16:36 | 121
Exodus 17 | 127
Exodus 18 | 135
Exodus 19 | 140
Exodus 20:1–11 | 146
Exodus 20:12–21 | 152
Exodus 21:1–11 | 157
Exodus 21:12–36 | 164
Exodus 22:1–15 | 170
Exodus 22:16—23:9 | 177
Exodus 23:10–31 | 183
Exodus 24 | 189

Conclusion | 195
Bibliography | 199

Introduction

God's Powerful Rescue, Covenant Journey, and the Human Condition

We're about to embark on an incredible journey through the opening chapters of the book of Exodus, specifically focusing on the pivotal narrative contained within Exod 1 through 24. These chapters are more than just ancient stories; they're a dynamic and powerful account of God's redemptive work in history, a testament to his unwavering commitment to his people. We'll be tracing the dramatic unfolding of God's rescue of the Israelites, a people who were once enslaved and oppressed, and witness their transformative encounter with Yahweh at the foot of Mount Sinai. While the entire book of Exodus is a monumental witness to God's character and power, our focus will be on this initial, crucial phase: the mighty acts of liberation and the establishment of the covenant relationship that would forever shape Israel's identity and mission. This study, born from years of engaging with the intricate connections between theology, culture, and economics at the Acton Institute here in Grand Rapids, and enriched by the privilege of teaching biblical interpretation and theological reflection to students at Kuyper College, seeks to illuminate the enduring relevance of these foundational chapters for our understanding of God, humanity, and the world he seeks to redeem.

Exodus 1–24 is far more than a simple record of historical events or a mere prelude to later developments in Israel's story. It stands as a vibrant theological declaration in its own right, revealing the very heart of the covenant-keeping God who hears the cries of the oppressed and intervenes decisively against seemingly insurmountable human power structures. Picking up the narrative thread directly from the promises made to Abraham in Genesis, these chapters plunge us into the harsh reality of Israel's plight in

Egypt—a people blessed by God, yet suffering under a regime explicitly hostile to God's purposes (Exod 1). The stage is thus set, not merely for a story of social liberation but for a cosmic conflict: the assertion of Yahweh's sovereignty against the defiant autonomy of Pharaoh and the oppressive systems he represents. God's intervention, therefore, is not a generalized act of goodwill, but a specific, covenantally-driven action to reclaim his people, the descendants of Abraham, Isaac, and Jacob, in fulfillment of his ancient promises and for the advancement of his global redemptive plan.

As we journey through these chapters, whether in personal study, Sunday-school classes, or small-group settings, we'll discover how these stories speak to our lives today. We'll see a God who is deeply concerned with the suffering of his people, a God who acts powerfully to liberate them from oppression. We'll find lessons of hope, courage, and unwavering faith, even in the face of seemingly impossible odds.

The narrative core of Exod 1–14 details this astonishing process of liberation. We witness God's meticulous preparation through the preservation and calling of Moses (Exod 2–4), followed by the escalating series of plagues unleashed upon Egypt (Exod 5–12). These are not random calamities but targeted judgments, systematically dismantling the political, economic, religious, and ecological pillars of Egyptian power, demonstrating Yahweh's absolute authority over every sphere claimed by Pharaoh and his gods. The institution of the Passover (Exod 12–13) becomes the defining ritual of redemption, sealing God's deliverance through substitutionary sacrifice and marking Israel as his protected people. This mighty act culminates in the miraculous crossing of the Red Sea (Exod 14)—a foundational event etched forever into Israel's memory as the ultimate demonstration of God's power to save his people and judge their oppressors. This entire sequence underscores God's unwavering commitment to his people and his fierce opposition to the forces arrayed against his plan.

Imagine the Israelites, trapped in the harsh reality of slavery, their cries rising to heaven. God, the covenant-keeping God, hears their cries and remembers his promises. He raises up Moses, an unlikely leader, and empowers him to confront Pharaoh, the most powerful ruler of his time. Through a series of dramatic plagues, God demonstrates his power and authority, not only over the gods of Egypt but over the very forces of nature. The Passover, a poignant reminder of God's saving grace, marks the turning point, as God's judgment passes over those marked by the blood of the lamb. And then, the climactic moment: the parting of the Red Sea, a breathtaking display of God's power and a symbol of his complete and utter deliverance.

These stories are not just historical accounts; they are powerful illustrations of God's character and his unwavering love for his people. They teach us that God is a God who hears the cries of the oppressed, a God who acts decisively to rescue his people, a God who is faithful to his promises. They remind us that no matter how dire our circumstances may seem, God is always present, always powerful, and always ready to deliver us.

However, liberation from bondage is immediately followed by the continued journey toward covenant relationship and holy living. The wilderness period, chronicled in chapters 15–18, serves as a crucial transition, preparing Israel for their encounter with God at Sinai. It is here that the murmuring and testing of Israel reveal the challenges of living in dependence upon God, even after experiencing his miraculous deliverance. The provision of manna and water, the victory over Amalek—these are not merely survival stories, but lessons in trusting God's provision and leadership.

As we read these chapters, we see the Israelites, fresh from their miraculous deliverance, struggling to adjust to their newfound freedom. They face hunger, thirst, and the constant threat of enemies. Yet, through it all, God remains faithful, providing for their needs and guiding them through the wilderness. These stories teach us that even after experiencing God's deliverance, we still face challenges and temptations. They remind us that true freedom is not just about being released from physical bondage, but also about learning to trust God and depend on him for our daily needs.

The climax of Exod 1–24 is undoubtedly the covenant establishment at Mount Sinai (Exod 19–24). This section, a veritable cornerstone of biblical theology, details God's self-revelation to Israel, the giving of the Ten Commandments, and the establishment of the Mosaic covenant. This covenant, far from being a mere legal code, is a relational document, defining the terms of Israel's unique relationship with Yahweh. It is here that Israel is constituted as God's chosen people, a "kingdom of priests and a holy nation" (Exod 19:6), tasked with reflecting God's character to the world. The detailed instructions for the construction of the tabernacle (Exod 25–31), while falling slightly outside our strict focus on Exod 1–24, are nonetheless foreshadowed in these chapters, hinting at God's desire to dwell among his people.

At Mount Sinai, God reveals himself to Israel in a powerful and awe-inspiring way. He descends upon the mountain in fire and smoke, his voice thundering across the landscape. He gives them the Ten Commandments, a moral compass for their lives, and establishes a covenant with them, a sacred agreement that defines their relationship with him. This covenant is not just a set of rules; it is an invitation to a deep and intimate relationship with God, a relationship that is based on love, trust, and obedience. It's an expression of what it means to love God and others.

As we explore these chapters, we will discover the heart of God's plan for his people. We will see how he desires to dwell among them, to guide them, and to bless them. We will learn that true covenant relationship with God is not about following a set of rules, but about living in a way that reflects his character and his love.

Through this detailed examination of Exod 1–24, we seek not only to understand the historical context of Israel's liberation and covenant formation, but also to grasp the enduring theological significance of these events. The God revealed in Exodus is a God who hears the cries of the oppressed, acts decisively to redeem his people, and establishes a covenant that defines their identity and mission. It is our hope that this study, rooted in years of reflection and engagement with the text in the context of both the Acton Institute and Kuyper College, will illuminate the timeless truths of these foundational chapters and inspire a deeper appreciation for the God who continues to redeem and restore his creation.

In our personal lives, in our church communities, and in our small groups, these stories will resonate with us on a profound level. We will see ourselves in the Israelites, struggling with doubt, fear, and temptation. We will witness God's power to deliver us from our own Egypt, our own bondage. And we will discover the beauty and the joy of a covenant relationship with the God who loves us and calls us to be his people. May this study be a journey of discovery, a journey of faith, and a journey of transformation.

This study guide will weave the insights of Gerard Van Groningen, Abraham Kuyper, Karen Horney, and Reinhold Niebuhr, and connect Exod 1–24 to personal, ecclesial, and societal issues. Bringing all of their insights together offers a unique opportunity for interpretation and application of Exodus contemporary life. Gerard Van Groningen, in his comprehensive work on messianic revelation, highlights how Exodus foreshadows the ultimate redemptive work of Christ. He emphasizes the continuity of God's saving acts, from the deliverance of Israel to the salvation offered through Jesus. As we study Exodus, we'll see how God's patterns of liberation and covenant making point toward the greater redemption achieved in Christ. Abraham Kuyper, with his emphasis on sphere sovereignty, reminds us that God's authority extends to every aspect of life. In Exodus, we witness God's sovereignty over the political, economic, and social structures of Egypt. Kuyper's insights help us understand how God's redemptive work is not limited to individual salvation but also impacts the broader societal context. We'll explore how Exodus challenges us to apply God's principles of justice and righteousness to our own communities and nations. Karen Horney, the psychoanalyst, explored the human struggle with anxiety and the search for security. Her insights resonate with the Israelites' experience in Exodus. Their enslavement, their fear of Pharaoh, and their journey through the wilderness reflect the human longing for safety and belonging. As we study Exodus, we'll see how God addresses these deep-seated human needs by providing deliverance, security, and a covenant relationship. Reinhold Niebuhr, the theologian and ethicist, grappled with the problem of sin and the complexities of human nature. His concept of "moral man and immoral society"[1] helps us understand the systemic nature of oppression in Egypt. Pharaoh's hardened heart and the oppressive structures he maintained reflect the reality of collective sin. In Exodus, we witness God's judgment against the oppression of his people and his call for a more righteous society.

(1) Personal Application—Exodus 1–24 speaks directly to our personal struggles with bondage, whether it's addiction, fear, or patterns of sin. We see God's willingness to hear our cries and his power to deliver us. The story of Moses reminds us that God can use flawed individuals to accomplish his purposes. The wilderness journey teaches us the importance of trusting God's provision and guidance in our daily lives.

(2) Church Application—For the church, Exodus serves as a model of God's redemptive work and the formation of a covenant community. The Passover reminds us of the power of Christ's sacrifice and the importance of remembering God's saving acts. The covenant at Sinai challenges us to live as a holy nation, reflecting God's character to the world.

(3) Social Application—Exodus calls us to confront injustice and care for our neighbors in need, especially within the community of God's people. The story of Israel's liberation reminds us that God is with his people and calls us to extend justice, mercy, and righteousness to others in response to his grace. The covenant principles, including the Ten Commandments, provide a moral foundation for living faithfully and building a free and virtuous community.

To aid us in this journey, each section of this study will be organized with subheadings designed to illuminate the narrative and its theological significance. However, it's important to note that the subheadings will develop organically throughout the book, reflecting the unique contours of each section. You'll find that the categories and number of subheadings may differ from one part of the study guide to another, as we seek to capture the specific themes and nuances present in each portion of Exod 1–24. We will pay close attention to the historical context, the literary structure, and the overarching themes that emerge from each passage, allowing the text itself to guide our exploration. Furthermore, we will include *Application Today* sections designed to bridge the gap between the ancient text and our contemporary lives. These sections will provide practical insights and reflective questions, encouraging us to consider how the truths of Exod 1–24 speak to

---

1. Niehbur, *Moral*, 200–278.

our personal struggles, our church communities, and the broader societal challenges we face. We will explore how God's acts of liberation, his establishment of covenant, and his revelation of his character can inform our understanding of justice, redemption, and our calling to be his people in the world today. By engaging with both the historical and the contemporary implications of these chapters, we aim to uncover the enduring relevance of Exod 1–24 for our lives and our communities.

Exodus 1–24 is not just a historical narrative; it's a living word that speaks to our personal struggles, our ecclesial responsibilities, and our societal challenges. As we journey through these chapters, may we encounter the God who redeems, restores, and transforms, and may we be inspired to live as his covenant people in a world that desperately needs his love and justice.

Key Themes from Gerard Van Groningen

Gerard Van Groningen (1921–2014) was a Dutch Reformed theologian and biblical scholar deeply rooted in the tradition of covenant theology. He served as a professor of Old Testament at Covenant Theological Seminary and was widely respected for his ability to integrate biblical theology with redemptive history. His major work *From Creation to Consummation* offers a sweeping vision of God's covenantal purposes from Genesis to Revelation, emphasizing God's glory as the central aim of creation and redemption.

Van Groningen's theology is marked by three foundational themes: covenant, kingdom, and mediator. These themes provide a robust framework for understanding the book of Exodus, which he saw not simply as a record of deliverance but as the unfolding of God's redemptive plan for his people and creation. His insights help modern readers see how Exodus builds upon Genesis—where God establishes his glory in time and history through creation—and prepares the way for the fulfillment of that glory in Christ.

In *From Creation to Consummation*, Gerard Van Groningen does a masterful job of setting the stage of our walk through the book of Exodus. Our goal will be the movement of God's grace in the life of his people for their good and God's glory. Exodus is a covenant book for a covenant people. The book presupposes some basic points from the book of Genesis. According to Van Groningen, Genesis tells the story of the setting of God's glory in time and history—namely, creation. The cosmos is the kingdom.[2] A kingdom involves a person, a king or queen who has supreme authority of the realm. A kingdom involves the actual exercise of royal authority. It is God himself who has sole, supreme authority of this creation. As we'll see

---

2. Van Groningen, *Creation*, 37.

in the book of Exodus, God has three purposes for his kingdom: (1) the cosmic kingdom makes known the will of God and how it is to be expressed in terms of the patterns and laws God implanted in his creation; (2) it also provides a setting for God to demonstrate the wonders and mysteries of life; and (3) it was to provide a home, a work and resting place for God's climactic creation, his image-bearers.[3] God created male and female to be his vicegerents. They were purposed to have a superior role, a dominant influence, and a responsible service.[4] Man and woman were created as more than mere creatures. They were to have a covenantal bond of life and love between God and themselves. Humanity was not created for the purpose of redemption. Creation was developed for the free exercise of "regal prerogatives and responsibilities that would bring to the highest and fullest extent the majesty, grandeur, and glory of God and, as a correlate to that, the full realization of honor, joy, and peace of mankind."[5]

Man and woman were called to three covenant mandates: (1) the cultural mandate where man and woman were to exercise their royal prerogatives by ruling over, developing, and simultaneously maintaining the cosmos; (2) they were given the social mandate because God created them in his image and likeness as male and female. In order to carry out the mandate they were to be fruitful, as married parents, in raising children; (3) they were given a fellowship mandate. They were expected to remain in close and intimate relationship with him and honoring him by doing what they were instructed to do.[6] And, as we learn in Genesis chapter 3, all this goodness was sabotaged by the fall.

Van Groningen rightly reminds us that "the fall" is not the best way to describe what happened in Gen 3. Phrases like "deviation," "transgression," or "breaking over the covenant" are better ways of describing what actually happened during that tragic event.[7] The garden of Eden was humanity's home. It was the place where Adam and Eve were to live out their royal status as covenant vicegerents, living out the cultural, social, and fellowship mandates. They were placed in the garden with limitations on their authority to decide for themselves the definition of what is true, good, and beautiful. That sort of knowledge was set aside for the creator alone. Theirs was not a covenant of works, which would render them worthy of God's grace because of their meritorious works.[8] Theirs was a covenant of grace

3. Van Groningen, *Creation*, 40.
4. Van Groningen, *Creation*, 59.
5. Van Groningen, *Creation*, 60.
6. Van Groningen, *Creation*, 68.
7. Van Groningen, *Creation*, 96.
8. Van Groningen, *Creation*, 98.

governed by God's goodness for them as covenant people. It was a bond of life and love and it was sabotaged by the serpent. Evil and sin entered Eden and changed the course of human history through Adam and Eve going rogue and breaking the covenant that God made with them. The serpent deceived Eve, Adam did not intervene, and they broke covenant and plunged humanity into an existence of assuming autonomous knowledge apart from God. The spiritual forces of evil captured the hearts of humankind, curses were pronounced, and eventually the kingdom of Satan, using its limited powers and forces, established itself in direct opposition to Yahweh and of all of the mediators established to represent God's people, including Christ.[9] The kingdom of Satan is a parasitic kingdom because it depends on creation for its existence.[10] Satan is totally dependent on the cosmic kingdom of Yahweh and has limitations on his activities, only going so far as the sovereign God allows. The parasite king, Satan, seeks to gain control of the hearts and minds of God's people and seeks to sabotage the plans that God has for his people. The parasitic kingdom and its developing influence is its own narrative in the book of Exodus.

The "Golden Cable" is a theological framework developed by Gerard Van Groningen to provide a cohesive understanding of the Bible's overarching narrative. Rather than centering on redemption alone, Van Groningen identifies three key strands—covenant, kingdom, and mediator—as the golden threads that run throughout Scripture and bind it into a unified whole. This framework offers a deeply relational, historical, and Christ-centered lens through which to interpret God's dealings with humanity. By tracing these three interwoven themes across the biblical storyline, Van Groningen highlights how God's sovereign purposes are progressively revealed and ultimately fulfilled in Jesus Christ.

In Van Groningen's theology, covenant represents the relationship between God and his people, and it is foundational to understanding how God interacts with humanity throughout Scripture. The covenant is established by God and is central to his dealings with his creation, beginning with Adam and continuing through figures such as Noah, Abraham, Moses, and David, ultimately being fulfilled in Christ. The covenant reflects both God's promises to his people and the expectations he sets for their obedience and faithfulness.

In the Golden Cable, the covenant serves as the bond that ties God's people to him, across all generations, reinforcing the idea that God is faithful to his promises and his people, even in the face of human sinfulness. Van

---

9. Van Groningen, *Creation*, 103.
10. Van Groningen, *Creation*, 103–4.

Groningen emphasizes the ongoing nature of God's covenantal relationship, where he progressively reveals his redemptive plan throughout history. The kingdom is the realm over which God rules as sovereign king. From the creation of the cosmos to the eschatological hope of the new creation, God's kingdom is central to Van Groningen's framework. The kingdom encompasses all of creation, with God exercising his supreme authority, and this concept unfolds throughout the narrative of Scripture. In the biblical story, God's kingdom is revealed in stages: in Eden (where Adam and Eve were vicegerents), through the formation of Israel (God's people as a theocratic nation under his law), and in the New Testament through the coming of Christ (the inauguration of the kingdom of God). Van Groningen sees the kingdom as the sphere where God's rule is exercised, and it is an essential element of understanding how God's purposes for creation are realized. The mediator is the one through whom God's kingdom and covenant are realized. Van Groningen emphasizes that throughout redemptive history, God raises up mediators to accomplish his purposes. In the Old Testament, these mediators included figures like Adam, Noah, Abraham, Moses, and David—each serving a role in mediating God's covenant and rule to his people.

Ultimately, Jesus Christ is the final and perfect mediator of the new covenant, fulfilling the roles of prophet, priest, and king. As the God-Man, Christ mediates between God and humanity, bringing the promises of the covenant to their fulfillment, establishing God's kingdom, and providing access to the Father. His mediatorship is essential for understanding how God's kingdom is brought to fruition through the work of salvation.

Summary of the Golden Cable Framework

- Covenant: The relational bond between God and his people, unfolding throughout Scripture.
- Kingdom: God's sovereign rule over all creation, progressively revealed throughout history.
- Mediator: The appointed figures (culminating in Christ) who serve as the means through which God's kingdom and covenant are brought to completion.

This Golden Cable binds the biblical narrative together by showing the interconnectedness of covenant, kingdom, and mediator. These themes run through every aspect of Scripture, forming the unified story of God's redemptive purposes for his people and his creation.

Key Themes from Reinhold Niebuhr

Reinhold Niebuhr (1892–1971) was one of the most influential American theologians and public intellectuals of the twentieth century. A pastor, professor, and social ethicist, Niebuhr is best known for his work on the nature of human sin, responsibility, and the complexities of moral action in public life. His thought blended theological depth with philosophical realism, especially in grappling with the tensions of human nature. Central to Niebuhr's theological anthropology is the idea that anxiety is the precondition for sin. While not itself sinful, anxiety arises from the human condition—being both finite and self-aware—which creates a profound sense of vulnerability and insecurity. According to Niebuhr, it is how individuals respond to this anxiety that leads either toward faith in God or toward sinful attempts at control or escape. This framework forms a powerful lens through which to understand the moral and spiritual struggles of human life. Reinhold Niebuhr's claim that anxiety is the precondition for sin refers to the idea that human beings, by virtue of their finite and limited nature, live in a state of inherent tension and insecurity. This existential anxiety arises because humans are both creatures with limited power and knowledge, and beings who possess self-awareness, enabling them to recognize their limitations, vulnerabilities, and mortality. Niebuhr believed that this anxious awareness creates the conditions in which sin becomes possible.

The Nature of Human Anxiety

Niebuhr views anxiety as an unavoidable part of human existence. Humans are finite beings, constrained by their physical and intellectual limitations. Yet, unlike other creatures, humans possess the capacity for self-reflection and awareness of their mortality and limitations. This combination of being finite and knowing one is finite generates anxiety. Humans feel exposed and vulnerable in a world that they cannot fully control or comprehend. Niebuhr describes anxiety as a neutral condition—it is not sinful in itself, but it creates the potential for sin. This anxiety becomes the precondition for sin because humans are inclined to try to alleviate their discomfort by exercising control over their circumstances in ways that may violate their relationship with God and others. Niebuhr believed that human beings typically respond to existential anxiety in one of two ways: pride (the attempt to become self-sufficient and control one's environment) or sensuality (the abandonment of responsibility by indulging in immediate pleasures).[11]

---

11. Niebuhr, *Destiny*, 186–203.

Both of these responses reflect a failure to trust in God and a turning away from humility, dependence, and faith.

Pride (Self-Sufficiency)

In their attempt to alleviate anxiety, humans often grasp for control and power. This is the sin of pride. Rather than trusting in God's provision and guidance, humans seek to become autonomous, believing that they can secure their own fate and overcome their vulnerability. This desire for self-sufficiency is an expression of hubris and rebellion against the limits of human nature, leading to sinful behaviors like exploitation, domination, and disregard for others in the pursuit of control. Niebuhr argued that pride is the most fundamental of sins because it arises from an attempt to place oneself in the role of God, denying one's creaturely limitations. By seeking to overcome anxiety through power and control, humans fall into the trap of self-worship and reject their dependence on God.

Sensuality (Self-Abandonment)

On the other hand, some individuals respond to anxiety by succumbing to sensuality—seeking escape from the burden of responsibility and freedom by immersing themselves in physical pleasures or distractions. This response reflects an attempt to ignore or avoid the existential realities of life, rejecting the call to live faithfully in an uncertain world. Sensuality, for Niebuhr, is a form of escapism. Rather than confronting the tensions of life through faith in God, individuals may attempt to numb their anxiety by indulging in self-destructive behavior, seeking comfort in material pleasures, or immersing themselves in distractions. This, too, is a sinful response, as it avoids the responsibility of living a life in relationship with God and neighbor.

Anxiety, Freedom, and Responsibility

One of Niebuhr's key insights is that human anxiety is linked to human freedom. Because humans are free to make choices, they are also responsible for those choices. However, with this freedom comes the burden of responsibility, and with responsibility comes anxiety. People are anxious because they have the freedom to make decisions, and they are aware that their decisions have consequences. Niebuhr suggests that humans often find this burden too heavy to bear, leading to the temptation to avoid responsibility by either asserting control (pride) or fleeing into irresponsibility (sensuality). In both cases, humans are failing to live in faith, instead trusting in their own strength or seeking escape from their condition. Sin, therefore, is the attempt to relieve the tension of freedom and responsibility in ways that violate one's proper relationship with God and others.

Niebuhr argues that the proper response to anxiety is faith in God. Rather than attempting to overcome their vulnerabilities through prideful self-reliance or escaping through sensuality, humans are called to live in trust and dependence on God. Faith provides the means by which humans can face their anxiety without succumbing to sin. It allows individuals to embrace their limitations, trusting that God's providence and grace are sufficient to sustain them, even in the face of uncertainty and insecurity. Faith also redirects the human response to anxiety away from self-centered actions and toward love and service to others. Rather than seeking power over others or indulging in self-gratification, faith compels individuals to live in humility and solidarity, recognizing their shared dependence on God. At the heart of Niebuhr's theology is the notion that sin, in all its forms, is ultimately a failure to trust in God. Whether it is the prideful attempt to control one's destiny or the escapist pursuit of pleasure, sin reflects a rejection of the security and peace that comes from relying on God. Instead, humans seek to secure their own existence on their terms, resulting in alienation from God, from others, and from themselves.

In this sense, anxiety is the condition that exposes the human tendency to distrust God and turn inward in selfishness or fear. It is not anxiety itself that is sinful, but the failure to meet that anxiety with faith and trust in God's provision. Niebuhr's understanding of anxiety as the precondition for sin can be illustrated through various biblical narratives. In the garden of Eden (Gen 3), Adam and Eve's fear of missing out on knowledge and control leads them to sin. Instead of trusting in God's command, they reach for self-sufficiency, which results in their separation from God. Similarly, in the story of Cain and Abel (Gen 4), Cain's anxiety about his acceptance before God leads him to murder his brother in a sinful attempt to assert control over his own standing. Throughout the Bible, the tension between faith in God and reliance on oneself is a central theme. Trusting in God, rather than attempting to control or escape from life's difficulties, is consistently portrayed as the path to righteousness.

Reinhold Niebuhr's insight that anxiety is the precondition for sin emphasizes the human condition of vulnerability and the temptation to overcome it in ways that lead to rebellion against God. Human anxiety, while not sinful in itself, provides the conditions for sin by prompting humans to seek control or escape apart from faith in God. Pride and sensuality are two primary responses to this anxiety, both of which are sinful because they represent a failure to trust in God's sovereignty and grace. The antidote to anxiety is faith—a faith that acknowledges human limitations, embraces the uncertainties of life, and relies on God's sustaining presence rather than human effort or understanding.

Key Themes from Karen Horney

Karen Horney (1885–1952) was a German-born psychoanalyst who broke with classical Freudian theory after immigrating to the United States, pioneering a cultural and relational approach to neurosis. Her signature concept of basic anxiety—the childhood fear of helplessness in a hostile world—yielded three coping styles: moving toward, against, or away from others. These lenses illuminate the book of Exodus: Pharaoh's brutal need to dominate (against), Moses's oscillation between self-doubt and courageous advocacy (toward and eventually against), and Israel's repeated retreats into complaint or idol making (away) all read as strategies for mastering collective insecurity. Horney thus offers a psychologically coherent map for understanding how fear, power, and the longing for safety drive every major figure in the Exodus drama.

Basic anxiety, according to Karen Horney, is a fundamental concept in her psychoanalytic theory.[12] It refers to the deep feeling of insecurity and fear that a child experiences when they perceive themselves as helpless in a potentially hostile world. Horney believed that this anxiety arises primarily from disturbances in the child's relationships with their caregivers, especially if the caregivers are indifferent, overprotective, or inconsistent in providing security and affection.

Basic anxiety results from unmet needs for safety, love, and belonging, which lead to feelings of loneliness, helplessness, and fear of abandonment. According to Horney, children develop coping strategies to deal with this anxiety, which may manifest as moving toward others (seeking approval or affection), moving against others (aggressively seeking control), or moving away from others (withdrawing emotionally). These patterns, if solidified in childhood, can influence personality development and interpersonal relationships in adulthood. Horney's idea of basic anxiety highlights the importance of early nurturing relationships and their impact on emotional and psychological health. Karen Horney introduced the concepts of self-expansive, self-effacing, and self-resignation as part of her analysis of neurotic

---

12. Horney, *Neurosis*, 17–18.

coping strategies in response to anxiety and insecurity.[13] These strategies reflect different ways people relate to themselves and others to alleviate their internal conflicts. Here's an explanation of each:

Self-Expansive

The self-expansive type is characterized by an aggressive and dominant approach to life. Individuals with this tendency seek power, recognition, and achievement to compensate for feelings of inadequacy or insecurity. They believe that expanding their influence and control over others will alleviate their anxiety and make them feel valuable. This often manifests in an outward display of confidence, ambition, and sometimes hostility. They tend to move against others, driven by a need for superiority, success, and independence.

Key traits:

- Need for achievement, power, and control
- Focus on personal success and recognition
- Can be competitive or domineering in relationships

Self-Effacing

The self-effacing type is marked by a tendency to subordinate oneself to others. These individuals cope with their anxiety by seeking love, affection, and approval through submission and self-sacrifice. They move toward others, believing that if they are likable, humble, and accommodating, they will receive the care and attention they crave. This coping style often involves self-denial, compliance, and an overemphasis on pleasing others.

Key traits:

- Desire for love, approval, and acceptance
- Tendency toward self-sacrifice and people pleasing
- May suppress their own needs to maintain harmony

---

13. Horney, *Neurosis*, 187–290.

Self-Resignation

The self-resignation type involves withdrawing from others and from life's demands. People who adopt this strategy tend to move away from others, seeking detachment, isolation, or emotional withdrawal as a means of coping with their anxiety. They may give up on personal goals or relationships, preferring to live in resignation, believing they cannot achieve or connect meaningfully with others. This results in an attitude of apathy, passivity, and avoidance.

Key traits:

- Withdrawal from relationships and responsibilities
- Apathy or passivity toward life goals
- Preference for isolation and emotional distance

Summary:

- Self-expansive types move against others to assert control and superiority.
- Self-effacing types move toward others to gain affection and approval.
- Self-resignation types move away from others, seeking emotional withdrawal and detachment.

These patterns are seen as ways individuals cope with the fundamental anxieties and conflicts they experience, especially in neurotic personalities.

Karen Horney's concept of the idealized self refers to a neurotic individual's unrealistic, glorified image of who they think they should be, as opposed to who they actually are. This idealized self is a mental construct that embodies perfection and serves as a coping mechanism for deep-seated feelings of inadequacy, insecurity, and basic anxiety. Horney believed that people develop this idealized image to escape the pain of self-doubt and to compensate for their perceived flaws.

Key Features of the Idealized Self

1. Unrealistic standards: The idealized self is a version of oneself that is built on impossible ideals of perfection, success, or virtue. It is not grounded in the person's real capacities or traits but rather reflects an exaggerated and unattainable version of who they think they should be.

2. Disconnection from the real self: The individual becomes alienated from their real self, which includes both their strengths and weaknesses. Instead of embracing their authentic self, they strive to become this idealized image, leading to inner conflict.

3. Tyranny of the "shoulds": Horney identified that individuals with an idealized self are often driven by rigid demands and expectations of themselves, known as the "tyranny of the shoulds." They constantly feel they should be more successful, more attractive, more intelligent, more virtuous, etc. This creates an internal pressure to live up to this idealized self-image, often resulting in frustration and feelings of failure.

4. Neurotic pride: Alongside the idealized self, individuals often develop a sense of neurotic pride, in which they derive a false sense of worth from their perceived alignment with their idealized self. This pride is fragile and conditional because it depends on living up to these unrealistic expectations.

5. Self-hate: When individuals inevitably fail to meet the standards of their idealized self, they experience feelings of guilt, shame, and self-hate. This internal self-criticism intensifies their insecurity and perpetuates the cycle of neurotic behavior.

The Role of the Idealized Self in Neurotic Conflict

Horney viewed the idealized self as central to neurosis because it leads to a constant struggle between a person's real self (authentic, but imperfect) and their idealized self (perfect, but unattainable). This conflict creates psychological distress and drives neurotic patterns of behavior, such as compulsive striving, people pleasing, or withdrawal. Karen Horney's idealized self represents a neurotic individual's attempt to cope with their deep feelings of inadequacy by creating an unrealistic, ideal version of themselves. This image becomes a source of inner conflict as they try to live up to impossible standards, often leading to frustration, self-criticism, and emotional turmoil. Reinhold Niebuhr's claim that anxiety is the precondition for sin highlights the inherent tension in human existence, where we recognize both our dependence on God and our freedom to make choices. Anxiety arises because humans are finite creatures who are aware of their vulnerabilities, limitations, and the uncertainties of life. In this state of anxiety, humans often face the temptation to alleviate these fears by exerting control or seeking security in their own abilities, power, or resources rather than trusting in God. This self-reliance, Niebuhr argues, is the root of sin. When humans act out of this anxiety without faith in God, they fall into pride, selfishness, or despair, all of which distance them from God.

Examples

In Exodus, Pharaoh's anxiety over losing control of the Israelite population leads to his oppressive actions and hardened heart. In Exod 1:9–10, Pharaoh expresses fear that the growing Israelite population may join his enemies and overthrow his kingdom. This fear leads to the enslavement of the Israelites and, later, to his refusal to obey God's commands through Moses, culminating in the plagues. Pharaoh's anxiety over his power leads him to resist God, trusting in his own might and rejecting God's sovereignty. This is an example of sin rooted in anxiety and self-reliance.

- Exodus 5:2: "Pharaoh said, 'Who is the Lord, that I should obey him and let Israel go? I do not know the Lord and I will not let Israel go.'" Pharaoh's defiance reflects his reliance on his own power and refusal to trust in the higher authority of God.

Moses's Anxiety and Trust in Self

Moses, too, experiences anxiety that leads to a struggle with faith in God's plan. When God calls Moses to lead the Israelites out of Egypt, Moses is anxious about his own inadequacy. In Exod 4:10, Moses protests, saying, "Pardon your servant, Lord. I have never been eloquent . . . I am slow of speech and tongue." Moses's fear of failure and self-doubt show a lack of trust in God's ability to use him despite his weaknesses. God reassures Moses that he will be with him, but this exchange reveals Moses's human tendency to trust in his own perceived limitations instead of God's power.

- Exodus 4:13: "But Moses said, 'Pardon your servant, Lord. Please send someone else.'" Moses's reluctance reflects his anxiety about his inadequacy, and his initial resistance to God's call is a moment of self-reliance over faith.

The Israelites' Anxiety and Rebellion

The Israelites themselves exhibit anxiety throughout their journey in the wilderness, which often leads them to sin by rejecting God's provision and direction. After leaving Egypt, they quickly become anxious about food and water, complaining to Moses and expressing a desire to return to Egypt where they had physical security, even in slavery (Exod 16:3). Their anxiety over survival leads to mistrust of God's promises and guidance.

- Exod 32:1: "When the people saw that Moses was so long in coming down from the mountain, they gathered around Aaron and said, 'Come, make us gods who will go before us.'" The Israelites' anxiety about Moses's absence and the uncertainty of the future prompts them to commit the sin of idolatry, creating the golden calf.

In all these cases, anxiety leads the main characters in Exodus to sin by trusting in themselves rather than relying on God's plan. Pharaoh's anxiety over his kingdom's stability causes him to oppose God's will, while Moses's anxiety about his own capabilities makes him hesitant to fulfill his calling. The Israelites' anxiety over their survival leads them to rebel and seek comfort in false gods. Each instance highlights how anxiety can tempt individuals to take control of their situation in ways that distance them from God's provision and authority.

Niebuhr's insight about anxiety as the precondition for sin is clearly seen in Exodus, where both leaders and the people face existential uncertainty and fear. When they choose to rely on their own strength, they fall into sin. In contrast, when Moses ultimately places his trust in God, he is able to lead the Israelites toward their deliverance. The lesson of Exodus, in line with Niebuhr's theology, is that faith in God is the antidote to the destructive effects of anxiety. When we place our trust in God rather than in ourselves, we are freed from the anxiety that leads to sin and are empowered to follow God's will.

- Proverbs 3:5–6: "Trust in the LORD with all your heart and lean not on your own understanding; in all your ways submit to him, and he will make your paths straight."
- Philippians 4:6–7: "Do not be anxious about anything, but in every situation, by prayer and petition, with thanksgiving, present your requests to God. And the peace of God, which transcends all understanding, will guard your hearts and your minds in Christ Jesus."

Reinhold Niebuhr and Karen Horney offer complementary psychological and theological frameworks that enrich our understanding of the central figures in Exodus chapters 1 to 32. Niebuhr's perspective reveals how existential anxiety arising from human limitations prompts characters like Pharaoh, Moses, and the Israelites to either assert prideful control or seek escapist comforts, distancing them from faith in God. Concurrently, Horney's insights into basic anxiety and neurotic coping strategies further clarify how these anxieties manifest in relational dynamics: Pharaoh exhibits self-expansion through domination, Moses initially leans toward self-resignation and withdrawal, and the Israelites oscillate between self-effacing dependence and self-resigning withdrawal in times of fear and uncertainty. Together, these approaches illuminate the psychological depth of Exodus, underscoring how anxiety—if unaddressed by faith and trust in God's provision—leads inevitably toward destructive behaviors and estrangement from authentic relationship with God and one another.

Key Themes from Abraham Kuyper

Abraham Kuyper (1837–1920) was a Dutch pastor-turned-newspaper-editor who founded the Free University of Amsterdam, organized a nationwide Christian political party, and eventually served as prime minister of the Netherlands. A theologian by training, he made the now-famous statement, "There is not a square inch in the whole domain of our human existence over which Christ, who is Sovereign over all, does not cry: Mine!"[14] Kuyper lambasted the secular liberalism he traced to the French Revolution, yet he also championed civil liberties, parliamentary democracy, and an energetic press—a blend often labeled Christian liberalism. Convinced that modernity's centrifugal forces would tear society apart, he advanced the doctrine of sphere sovereignty: family, church, state, and other spheres answer directly to God, not to one another, thereby preserving pluralism while restraining tyranny.

Those categories make Kuyper an incisive guide to the book of Exodus. Exodus narrates God's claim of sovereignty over Pharaoh, the liberation of a slave people, and the formation of a covenant community governed by just laws and social compassion. Kuyper's twin emphases—God's royal authority over every sphere and the demand for charity and justice in public life—mirror Exodus's movement from political deliverance to ethical nation building. Reading Moses through Kuyper's lens highlights both the danger of totalizing power and the divine mandate to build a society where every

14. Bratt, *Kuyper*, 488.

sphere, from household to state, upholds righteousness, the rule of law, and neighbor love.

Abraham Kuyper's perspective on the social order, as explored by Matthew J. Tuininga, offers a rich theological framework that helps us interpret the themes of Exodus chapters 1-32.[15] Kuyper's emphasis on God's sovereignty over all spheres of life, the integration of justice and charity, and the rejection of both radical individualism and materialism can serve as a guide for understanding how God intervenes in human history in the Exodus narrative, and how these insights can shape the Christian approaches to social justice.

Kuyper's View of Sovereignty and Exodus

One of Kuyper's central tenets is that God's sovereignty extends over every square inch of creation. This idea aligns with the portrayal of God in the book of Exodus, where his sovereignty over the political, social, and spiritual realms of the Israelites' lives is vividly demonstrated. In Exodus, God confronts Pharaoh, a symbol of human sovereignty and empire, to liberate his people. The plagues (Exod 7-12), the parting of the Red Sea (Exod 14), and the giving of the law at Mount Sinai (Exod 19-20) all showcase God's supreme authority over creation, rulers, and nations. Kuyper's concept of sphere sovereignty, where different aspects of life—such as the state, the family, and the church—operate under God's rule, can be applied to the book of Exodus. The various challenges the Israelites face in their journey are not just personal or spiritual but encompass social, economic, and political realms. God's intervention is comprehensive, liberating the Israelites from slavery, providing laws to shape their communal life, and establishing principles for justice and worship.

Justice, Law, and the Ten Commandments

Kuyper's thought particularly resonates with the giving of the Ten Commandments in Exod 20. For Kuyper, the law is an expression of God's moral order for society. It serves as a foundation for justice and righteousness, not just a set of religious rituals. Similarly, in Exodus, God gives the law to Moses to create a just society where God's people live in alignment with his will. The commandments are not merely spiritual instructions; they are deeply social and communal. For instance, commandments related to honoring parents,

15. Tuininga, "Abraham Kuyper." 345-47.

refraining from theft, and respecting property rights are about maintaining justice and fairness within the community. This reflects Kuyper's view that social justice is at the heart of biblical ethics. The law is meant to guide the community in love, fairness, and equity—principles that Kuyper would argue are necessary for any Christian engagement with society.

The Diaconate and the Role of the Church

Kuyper's insistence on the church's role in addressing social needs echoes the role of Moses as both a spiritual and social leader of Israel. Just as Kuyper emphasized that the diaconate (church-based poor relief) was essential for addressing social crises, Moses serves as a leader who mediates between God and the people, providing both spiritual guidance and practical laws to ensure the community's welfare. The laws given in Exod 21–23 outline principles for handling property, dealing with poverty, and maintaining justice—showing that God's concern extends to every aspect of life. For the modern church, Kuyper's understanding of the church's social responsibility, as seen through the lens of Exodus, calls believers to be deeply involved in promoting justice, supporting the poor, and creating communities where God's laws of love and justice are reflected. The church, like Israel, is called to be a community set apart, not just spiritually, but in the way it organizes its social life.

Kuyper's Critique of Materialism and Idolatry

Kuyper's critique of materialism and the idolatry of wealth can also be seen in the golden calf episode in Exod 32. The Israelites, anxious about their future, create a material idol to replace the invisible God who had liberated them from Egypt. Kuyper often warned against the idolatry of wealth, power, and material prosperity, and this story in Exodus illustrates the dangers of replacing God's sovereignty with human-made idols. The church today, guided by Kuyper's insights, can learn from this episode in Exodus about the dangers of idolatry in all its forms—whether it be wealth, status, or power. The church is called to reject such temptations and to remain faithful to God's commandments and his call to social justice.

Implications for the Modern Church

Kuyper's views on social justice, charity, and God's sovereignty provide a theological foundation for Christian mission today, much as they did for the Israelites in Exodus. Just as God called Israel to be a light to the nations through their obedience to his laws, Christians are called to reflect God's justice and mercy in every sphere of life. For Kuyper, this means God's people must be actively involved in promoting justice, caring for the poor, and ensuring that society reflects the moral order laid out in Scripture. In Exodus, God's deliverance of his people from slavery to freedom is both a physical and spiritual act, demonstrating that salvation encompasses all of life. Similarly, Kuyper argues that the gospel is not just about saving souls but about transforming every part of society. This comprehensive view of salvation, justice, and social order can empower churches today to take seriously their role in addressing social issues all while remaining grounded in God's sovereign rule. Overall, Kuyper's social theology enriches our understanding of the book of Exodus by highlighting how God's sovereignty, justice, and law are meant to shape not only individual lives but the entire structure of society. His emphasis on Christian responsibility to be socially engaged offers a model for how Christians today can live out the justice and compassion of God in a world that desperately needs both.

Conclusion

As we journey through Exod 1–24, we will rely on the theological and psychological insights of Gerard Van Groningen, Reinhold Niebuhr, Karen Horney, and Abraham Kuyper to illuminate the depth and relevance of the text. Van Groningen's covenantal framework reminds us that God's deliverance of Israel is not merely about rescue but about restoring his people to their identity and purpose under his kingship. Niebuhr exposes how anxiety—our fear of finitude—can become the root of sin when we grasp for control, a pattern seen in Pharaoh, the Israelites, and even Moses. Horney deepens this diagnosis by showing how basic anxiety and our learned coping strategies shape our relational behavior; Exodus reveals how domination, dependency, and withdrawal manifest under stress and divine testing. Kuyper's doctrine of sphere sovereignty shows that God's law is not confined to worship but extends to every area of life, calling his people to reject idolatry and live under his comprehensive lordship.

Together, these perspectives help us see Exodus not only as ancient history but as a living story of divine grace, justice, and transformation.

This is more than an academic study—it is an invitation to encounter the God who rescues, commands, dwells with, and reforms his people. May this encounter draw us into deeper trust, wholehearted obedience, and faithful witness to his glory in every sphere of life.

Exodus 1:1–14

Context and Analysis

This passage takes place after the death of Joseph and his generation, where a new Pharaoh rises to power who "did not know about Joseph" (Exod 1:8). The Israelites, having been fruitful and multiplied greatly as God commanded (Exod 1:7; cf. Gen 1:28), are now seen as a threat by the Egyptians. This leads Pharaoh to impose forced labor on the Israelites (Exod 1:11–14). Pharaoh responds to the growth of Israel with fear and oppression, seeking to control their population by enslaving them (Exod 1:9–11). The Israelites, despite their vulnerability under harsh conditions, continue to multiply and thrive (Exod 1:12), demonstrating resilience under God's hidden protection. Phrases like "multiplied" (Exod 1:7, 12) and "oppression" (Exod 1:11–13) are repeated, emphasizing the tension between God's blessing of the Israelites' fruitfulness and Pharaoh's fear-driven control. This contrast highlights the battle between divine providence and human fear.

Spiritual Insights: Basic Anxiety

Pharaoh's insecurity arises from fear that the Israelites' growing numbers will lead to rebellion (Exod 1:9–10). His anxiety leads to harsh oppression as a means of control (Exod 1:11). Pharaoh exhibits self-expansion, seeking power and dominance through slavery (Exod 1:11–13). The Israelites, enduring intense hardship, may feel a sense of self-resignation, yet they continue to multiply despite the oppression (Exod 1:12). Pharaoh, in his anxiety, trusts his own power and oppressive measures, but these lead to greater fear and injustice. In contrast, the Israelites' growth is a sign of God's providence and hidden work amidst their suffering (Exod 1:12).

Problems and Dilemmas

The oppression of the Israelites raises moral dilemmas of justice and power. Pharaoh's misuse of authority to enslave the Israelites reflects an abuse of power driven by fear (Exod 1:11–13). Pharaoh's idealized self is one of ultimate control and power, but, in reality, his actions reveal insecurity and weakness (Exod 1:9–10). He acts out of fear rather than moral leadership. This passage raises deeper questions about leadership, freedom, and God's plan. Why does God allow the Israelites to suffer, and how does this suffering fit into his larger redemptive plan for their deliverance (Exod 1:12)?

Themes and Obligations

Although the Israelites are vulnerable to Pharaoh's oppressive power, the text emphasizes that their numbers continued to grow, reflecting God's hidden protection and provision, even in the face of suffering (Exod 1:12). The Israelites' growth despite oppression challenges readers to reflect on resilience and faithfulness. It highlights God's ability to bless and strengthen his people even during times of intense hardship (Exod 1:7, 12). Pharaoh's fear and insecurity lead him to self-interest and harm, rather than noble leadership. His oppressive decisions, driven by fear, ultimately backfire as the Israelites continue to grow (Exod 1:12–13).

Reflections and Application

Like Pharaoh, modern individuals and societies may allow fear of losing control to lead to oppressive or unjust behaviors. The text invites us to reflect on how we respond to threats and challenges today, and whether we trust in God's sovereignty or resort to fear-driven actions (Exod 1:9–10). Pharaoh's desire for total control represents an unrealistic expectation of power. This passage challenges us to rely on God's sovereignty rather than trying to manipulate outcomes through fear or control (Exod 1:11–13).

Application Today: In leadership roles today, whether in business, politics, or personal life, the dangers of allowing fear to dictate decisions are evident. This passage calls for trust in God's providence and justice, rather than succumbing to the pressures of fear and control (Exod 1:9–10).

God's Sovereignty and Providence

Despite Pharaoh's best efforts to suppress the Israelites, God's purpose prevails as they continue to multiply (Exod 1:12). This underscores God's control over history and human rulers, reminding us to trust his ultimate plan (cf. Prov 19:21). Pharaoh's failure to recognize God's authority leads to injustice and suffering (Exod 1:9–11). This passage challenges both personal and societal leadership to submit to God's will, rather than relying on human efforts to secure control (cf. Ps 127:1).

Covenant Relationship and Faithfulness

Although not explicitly mentioned, God's covenant promise to Abraham, Isaac, and Jacob (cf. Gen 17:7–8) is evident in the multiplication and prosperity of the Israelites, even in difficult circumstances (Exod 1:7, 12). God remains faithful to his promises. This passage encourages readers to remain faithful during times of hardship, trusting that God's purposes are often worked out through suffering and difficulty (cf. Rom 8:28).

Human Vocation and Cultural Mandate

Despite their oppression, the Israelites continue to fulfill God's command to be fruitful and multiply (Exod 1:7; cf. Gen 1:28). Their growth reflects God's plan for them to fill the earth and reflects their obedience to the cultural mandate. This passage reminds us that even in difficult circumstances, we are called to continue in our work and service, trusting that God is at work even when we cannot see the results (cf. Col 3:23–24).

Common Grace and Resistance to Evil

Pharaoh represents the forces of evil and oppression (Exod 1:9–11), while the Israelites' fruitfulness reflects God's sustaining grace. Despite the suffering inflicted upon them, God's grace enables them to thrive (Exod 1:12). This passage challenges readers to consider how to resist evil in their own lives and communities. Even when unjust powers seem in control, we are called to trust in God's ultimate justice and act righteously (cf. Eph 6:13).

God's Grace and Redemptive History

The Israelites' growth in the face of Pharaoh's oppression points to God's redemptive plan for his people (Exod 1:12). This growth foreshadows the eventual deliverance that God will bring through Moses (Exod 3:7-10). This passage challenges us to trust that God is working out his plan of redemption, even when circumstances seem bleak or oppressive (cf. Isa 46:10).

Cultural Mandate and Kingdom Work

Despite being enslaved, the Israelites continue to multiply and grow, fulfilling God's cultural mandate to fill the earth (Exod 1:7, 12; cf. Gen 1:28). This reflects their participation in God's broader kingdom work, even in difficult circumstances. This passage reminds us that even in oppressive situations, we are called to be agents of renewal and participants in God's kingdom work (cf. Rom 8:19-23).

Social Mandate and Family Life

Pharaoh's oppression disrupts family and social structures, yet the Israelites continue to build families and communities despite the hardship (Exod 1:7, 12). This resilience reflects their trust in God's promises. This passage highlights the central role of families and communities in God's plan. It emphasizes that godly families are crucial to advancing God's purposes, even in the face of external threats (cf. Ps 127:3-5).

Liberty, Justice, and God's Kingdom

Pharaoh's oppression represents an unjust use of power, but the Israelites' continued growth points toward God's eventual plan for their liberation through Moses (Exod 3:7-10). God's justice will prevail. This passage calls us to pursue justice in our own contexts, standing against oppression and trusting that God will bring about his justice in his time (cf. Mic 6:8). In Exod 1:1-14, the Israelites face severe oppression under Pharaoh's rule. They are subjected to forced labor and economic exploitation, symbolizing the denial of their political and economic liberty. This reveals a deep injustice that cries out for God's intervention.

Spiritual Warfare

Pharaoh's fear leads him to oppressive actions (Exod 1:9–11), while the Israelites' resilience demonstrates faith and perseverance in the face of hardship (Exod 1:12). Their continued growth is a testament to God's faithfulness. This passage encourages us to stand firm in the face of moral and spiritual challenges, trusting in God's sovereignty and goodness (cf. Jas 1:2–4).

Questions for Reflection and Discussion

1. Pharaoh's actions are driven by fear of losing power (Exod 1:9–10). In what ways do we allow fear to drive our decisions today? How can we trust God more fully in areas where we feel powerless (cf. 2 Tim 1:7)?

2. Despite oppression, the Israelites continued to multiply (Exod 1:12). How can we trust in God's providence when we face difficulties or when situations seem beyond our control (cf. Rom 8:28)?

3. How can we, like the Israelites, maintain our integrity and faithfulness when faced with injustice or oppression in today's society? What does resisting evil look like in our daily lives (cf. Eph 6:10–12)?

4. Pharaoh's leadership is marked by fear and control (Exod 1:9–11). What lessons can we learn about godly leadership from this passage, especially in contexts of power and responsibility (cf. Matt 20:25–28)?

Exodus 1:15–22

Context and Analysis

Pharaoh, concerned by the growing number of Israelites, orders the Hebrew midwives Shiphrah and Puah to kill all male babies born to the Israelites (Exod 1:15–16). This command was motivated by fear that the Israelites would become too numerous and pose a threat to Egyptian power (Exod 1:9–10). The midwives, however, feared God and did not obey the king's command, choosing instead to let the boys live (Exod 1:17). To fear God means to hold him in the highest reverence, esteem, awe, honor, and glory. Pharaoh responds to his own insecurities with oppressive control, seeking to eliminate the perceived threat by murdering Israelite boys. In contrast, the Hebrew midwives respond with courage and defiance, trusting in God's authority over Pharaoh's power (Exod 1:17–19). The phrase "fear of God" (Exod 1:17, 21) highlights the key theme of divine authority versus human authority. The fear of God drives the midwives to disobey Pharaoh, showing their trust in a higher power. This contrast between Pharaoh's fear and the midwives' reverence for God underscores the tension between control and divine intervention.

Spiritual Insights: Basic Anxiety

Pharaoh's fear of losing control drives his actions (Exod 1:9–10). His anxiety about the growing strength of the Israelites leads to increasingly oppressive tactics. The Hebrew midwives, by contrast, likely experienced anxiety under the threat of Pharaoh's orders but chose to trust God over the fear of human consequences (Exod 1:17). Pharaoh seeks self-expansion through power and control, commanding the deaths of Israelite boys to preserve his reign (Exod 1:16). The midwives, however, display moral courage by trusting God and disobeying Pharaoh, acting out of fear of God rather than self-preservation (Exod 1:17). Pharaoh trusts in his own power, relying on brutal tactics to maintain control. The midwives, on the other hand, trust in God's sovereignty and protection, even at great personal risk (Exod 1:20–21). Their fear of God leads to their reward, as God blesses them with families of their own (Exod 1:21).

Problems and Dilemmas

The midwives face a profound moral dilemma—should they obey Pharaoh's command to kill or obey God's command to preserve life? Their choice to save the boys, even at personal risk, reflects their commitment to divine morality over human orders (Exod 1:17). Pharaoh's actions reveal a ruler trying to create an image of ultimate power, though his fear exposes his vulnerability. The midwives, by contrast, live authentically before God, prioritizing moral integrity over fear of punishment (Exod 1:17–19). This passage raises questions about allegiance and obedience. The midwives must choose between obedience to human authority or God's authority, a struggle that speaks to the broader conflict of where true power lies—human rulers or God (Exod 1:17–19).

Themes and Obligations

The midwives, though vulnerable under Pharaoh's rule, trust in God's protection. God blesses them for their faithfulness, demonstrating his care for those who fear him (Exod 1:20–21). Their actions remind readers that God is ultimately in control, even when human rulers seem powerful. This passage calls the reader to consider moral courage. The midwives' choice to protect life, rather than comply with evil, challenges readers to think about duty, justice, and what it means to act with nobility of character (Exod 1:17). The midwives pursue the noble goal of preserving life, standing in direct contrast to Pharaoh's self-interested desire for power and control (Exod 1:17–19). Their reverence for God and commitment to justice exemplify righteousness.

Reflections and Application

Pharaoh's fear-driven actions and the midwives' courage challenge modern readers to reflect on how they respond to fear and insecurity in their own lives. Do we, like Pharaoh, seek to control others out of fear, or do we, like the midwives, trust God in the face of opposition (Exod 1:9, 17)? Pharaoh's unrealistic desire for absolute control led to destructive and immoral decisions (Exod 1:16). This passage encourages reflection on how the pursuit of perfection or control can distort our moral judgment. In contrast, the midwives' faithfulness highlights the importance of prioritizing righteousness over power.

Application Today: In today's world, ethical dilemmas often arise where obedience to human laws or orders may conflict with God's commands. The midwives' defiance of unjust authority serves as a powerful model for how we can resist evil and stand for righteousness in personal, political, or social contexts (Exod 1:17).

God's Sovereignty and Providence

Despite Pharaoh's oppressive efforts, God's plan for Israel is not thwarted. The midwives' faithfulness leads to God's blessing, and the Israelite population continues to grow (Exod 1:20–21). This shows that God is sovereign over even the most powerful rulers. Pharaoh's refusal to acknowledge God's authority leads to his moral downfall, while the midwives' fear of God brings life and blessing. This passage challenges readers to recognize where true authority lies and to trust in God's ultimate control (Exod 1:20–21).

Covenant Relationship and Faithfulness

Although not explicitly stated, this passage reflects God's ongoing faithfulness to his covenant with Abraham, as he continues to protect and multiply the Israelites (Gen 17:2–6; Exod 1:20). The midwives' actions echo God's own faithfulness in preserving his people. The midwives' faithfulness to God, even at great personal risk, reminds readers of the importance of staying true to God's commands and trusting him for the outcome (Exod 1:17, 21). Their story encourages steadfastness in the face of opposition.

Human Vocation and Cultural Mandate

The midwives' calling to care for the vulnerable aligns with God's command to protect life. They fulfill their God-given vocation by protecting the children and honoring life (Exod 1:17). This passage emphasizes the importance of serving God with integrity in one's work, even when faced with difficult ethical choices. The midwives' actions demonstrate that all work, even in challenging circumstances, can honor God (Exod 1:20).

Common Grace and Resistance to Evil

Pharaoh represents the evil and oppressive forces of the world, while the midwives stand for God's goodness and justice (Exod 1:16–17). The passage highlights how God works through people who resist evil and uphold his values. The midwives' defiance of Pharaoh's orders demonstrates the importance of resisting evil, even when doing so comes at a personal cost. This passage encourages believers to stand for justice in the face of the oppression of God's people (Exod 1:17).

God's Grace and Redemptive History

The midwives' actions play a critical role in preserving the line of Israel, which would eventually lead to the birth of Moses, the deliverer of Israel (Exod 2:1–10). Their faithfulness becomes a part of God's larger redemptive plan.

Application Today: By trusting in God and preserving life, the midwives participate in God's redemptive plan for his people. This passage encourages us to see how our small acts of faithfulness can play a part in God's larger story of redemption (Exod 1:20–21).

Cultural Mandate and Kingdom Work

The midwives' decision to save the children allows the Israelites to continue multiplying, fulfilling God's original command to be fruitful and multiply (Gen 1:28; Exod 1:20). Their actions affirm God's plan for human flourishing, even in oppressive circumstances. The midwives' role in preserving life reflects their participation in God's kingdom work. Their story encourages us to act as agents of renewal in our own spheres of influence (Exod 1:17, 20).

Social Mandate and Family Life

By protecting the lives of Israelite boys, the midwives preserve family structures and ensure the growth of the Israelite community. Their actions highlight the importance of safeguarding family life in God's plan (Exod 1:17–21). The midwives' actions remind us of the critical role that women, families, and communities play in God's purposes. The progress of God's redemptive mission in the book of Exodus rests on the actions of God-honoring women, Their protection of life contributes to the continuation of God's people (Exod 1:21).

Liberty, Justice, and God's Kingdom

The midwives' decision to protect life represents a stand for justice against an oppressive ruler (Exod 1:17). Their actions model God's justice, revealing that his kingdom is characterized by life, protection, and liberation. The midwives' courage challenges us to pursue justice in our own lives, standing up for the vulnerable and resisting unjust authority (Exod 1:17). Exodus 1:15–22 highlights Pharaoh's cruelty through the decree to kill male Hebrew infants, an act of political control and genocide. God's justice is revealed in the midwives' defiance of this command, demonstrating that righteousness involves protecting life, even under oppressive political structures.

Spiritual Warfare

The midwives face the spiritual and moral challenge of choosing between obedience to God or Pharaoh. Their choice to preserve life demonstrates their integrity and spiritual courage (Exod 1:17). The midwives' refusal to comply with evil commands serves as a powerful reminder that we are called to stand firm in the face of moral challenges, trusting that God will honor our faithfulness (Exod 1:17, 21).

Questions for Reflection and Discussion

1. The Hebrew midwives feared God more than they feared Pharaoh (Exod 1:17). How does this passage challenge us to examine where our loyalties lie when faced with difficult decisions?

2. In what situations today might we be called to resist unjust authority or laws? How can we cultivate the kind of moral courage displayed by the midwives (Exod 1:17)?

3. Despite Pharaoh's oppression, God's plan for his people continued (Exod 1:20–21). How does this passage encourage us to trust God's sovereignty, even when circumstances seem overwhelming or unjust?

4. The midwives' decision to disobey Pharaoh's command raises questions about when we should prioritize obedience to God over human authority (Acts 5:29). How does this passage help guide us in making difficult decisions where obedience to God conflicts with societal or governmental demands?

Exodus 2:1–8

Context and Analysis

At this time, the Israelites were enslaved in Egypt under the oppressive rule of Pharaoh (Exod 1:11–14). Pharaoh had issued a decree that all Hebrew baby boys were to be killed at birth by throwing them into the Nile (Exod 1:22). Moses is born during this period of immense fear and danger. Moses's mother, Jochebed (later named in Exod 6:20), hides her son for three months (Exod 2:2), responding to Pharaoh's decree with quiet defiance. When she can no longer hide him, she places him in a basket in the Nile (Exod 2:3). Pharaoh's daughter discovers the child and chooses to protect him (Exod 2:6), while Moses's sister watches from a distance, showing concern and readiness to intervene (Exod 2:4–8). The term "basket" (Exod 2:3) is the same word used for Noah's ark (Gen 6:14), symbolizing salvation through water. The river, which was meant to be a place of death for Hebrew boys, becomes a place of divine intervention and protection for Moses.

Spiritual Insights: Basic Anxiety

Moses's family experiences deep anxiety and fear over the possibility of his discovery and death due to Pharaoh's decree (Exod 1:22). Jochebed's decision to hide him reflects her fear of losing her child, yet her ultimate action of placing him in the river shows both desperation and hope. Jochebed exhibits self-effacing behavior, acting with great care and submission to the situation but ultimately trusting in God by placing Moses in the basket (Exod 2:3). Pharaoh's daughter also shows empathy and disobedience to her father's command by choosing to save the child (Exod 2:6). Jochebed's actions reflect a blend of human fear and trust in God's providence. Instead of taking matters into her own hands through force, she places her trust in God's protection, releasing Moses into his care (Exod 2:3).

Problems and Dilemmas

The moral dilemma faced by Moses's mother involves a conflict between maternal love and obedience to Pharaoh's cruel command. Her decision to defy Pharaoh by hiding her son and then placing him in the Nile presents a tension between human action and trust in divine protection. Jochebed embodies the real self, acting in faith rather than trying to meet an idealized expectation of perfection or control over her son's fate (Exod 2:3). Her actions display a recognition of human limitation and the need for divine intervention. The passage raises questions about obedience to human authority versus moral integrity and faith in God. Moses's survival depends on the courageous actions of multiple women (his mother, his sister, and Pharaoh's daughter), highlighting the role of faith-driven disobedience to unjust laws.

Themes and Obligations

The theme of God's protection is central, as Moses is saved from certain death by a series of divinely orchestrated events. Human vulnerability is evident, but God's providential care transforms a dangerous situation into one of salvation (Exod 2:5–6). The characters in this passage demonstrate moral courage. Jochebed and Pharaoh's daughter both take significant risks to protect the life of a child. Their actions challenge readers to reflect on how we might show similar courage in standing against injustice (Exod 2:3, 6). The women in this passage pursue the noble goal of preserving life, even in the face of fear and danger. They do not allow self-interest or resignation to dictate their actions, but instead act selflessly and courageously (Exod 2:3–6).

Reflections and Application

Many today face overwhelming fears and situations beyond their control. Just as Jochebed had to release her son into the river, trusting God with the outcome, we, too, are called to relinquish control and trust in God's providence in times of fear and uncertainty (cf. Phil 4:6–7). Moses's mother likely struggled with letting go of the idealized vision of her son's safety. In our own lives, we often cling to unrealistic expectations, forgetting that faith sometimes requires us to release our plans and trust in God's protection (cf. Matt 6:25–34).

Application Today: In a leadership or community context, this passage challenges us to take risks to protect the vulnerable, trusting that God will guide and protect even in the face of overwhelming challenges. Like Jochebed and Pharaoh's daughter, we are called to courageously protect life (cf. Jas 1:27).

God's Sovereignty and Providence

The passage reveals God's providential care over Moses, working through the actions of faithful women to preserve the life of Israel's future deliverer (Exod 2:3–6). This highlights that even in a world of oppressive rulers, God's purposes prevail. Despite Pharaoh's attempts to suppress and destroy the Israelites, God's authority and plans cannot be thwarted. This passage reminds us to trust in God's sovereignty in both personal and societal leadership (cf. Rom 8:28).

Covenant Relationship and Faithfulness

Though not explicitly stated, God's covenant with Abraham, Isaac, and Jacob (cf. Gen 12:2–3) is being fulfilled through Moses's preservation. This passage shows God's faithfulness to his promises, even in dark times of oppression (Exod 2:2–3). This passage encourages believers to remain faithful, knowing that God is at work even in situations that seem hopeless or beyond control. Jochebed's faith in placing Moses in the basket is a testament to trusting God's providence (cf. Heb 11:23).

Human Vocation and Cultural Mandate

The women in this passage fulfill their vocations by protecting and nurturing life. Jochebed, Pharaoh's daughter, and Moses's sister all demonstrate their roles as caretakers, fulfilling God's call to preserve life (Exod 2:3–4, 6). This passage emphasizes the importance of serving others, particularly the vulnerable. Like these women, we are called to serve and care for those in need, trusting that our actions can be part of God's greater plan (cf. Gal 6:9–10).

Common Grace and Resistance to Evil

Pharaoh represents the forces of evil, while the actions of Jochebed and Pharaoh's daughter illustrate God's grace working to preserve Moses's life (Exod 2:3, 6). The Nile, which was meant for death, becomes a place of life through God's intervention. The quiet defiance of these women in the face of Pharaoh's evil decree challenges readers to consider how we too might resist evil and choose righteousness in our own contexts (cf. Eph 6:12).

God's Grace and Redemptive History

The preservation of Moses is a key moment in God's redemptive plan for Israel. Through this act of grace, God prepares the way for Moses to lead his people out of slavery (Exod 2:6-8). This passage foreshadows the ultimate deliverance that will come through Christ (cf. Matt 2:13-15). This passage encourages believers to recognize God's grace and intervention in their own lives, reminding us that even in difficult times, God is working toward redemption (cf. Eph 1:11).

Cultural Mandate and Kingdom Work

In Exod 2:1-8, we see the faithful stewardship of life in the face of political oppression. Moses's parents protect and nurture him, reflecting the biblical mandate to cultivate and preserve life (Gen 1:28). Despite Pharaoh's decree to kill all male Hebrew infants, Moses's mother places him in a basket on the Nile, trusting in God's providence to protect her son (Exod 2:3). This act of preservation aligns with the call to steward life and participate in God's creation even in hostile circumstances.

Application Today: This passage challenges us to engage in our work, calling with the same spirit of preservation and trust in God. In contexts where life is threatened—whether physically, socially, or spiritually—believers are called to protect, nurture, and develop creation in a way that honors God's kingdom purposes. In today's world, this can apply to efforts such as environmental stewardship, protecting vulnerable populations, and supporting life-affirming causes.

Social Mandate and Family Life

The story of Moses's early life in Exod 2:1-8 highlights the importance of family in preserving life and passing on faithfulness to God. Moses's parents defy the oppressive orders of Pharaoh, risking their own safety to protect their child. Moses's sister, Miriam, also plays a vital role in ensuring his safety (Exod 2:4, 7-8). This reflects the critical role of families in safeguarding children, teaching them faith, and preparing them to fulfill God's purposes.

Application Today: This passage teaches us about the centrality of family in advancing God's purposes. Godly families are foundational to raising future generations who trust in God's providence, even in the face of societal challenges. Believers today are called to support, nurture, and protect their families, ensuring that they grow in faith and fulfill their role in God's mission. Communities of faith can also play a role in supporting families through challenging times.

Liberty, Justice, and God's Kingdom

In this passage, God's concern for justice is displayed through his preservation of Moses, who will later become the deliverer of Israel. Although the political and social environment is unjust, as seen through Pharaoh's oppressive laws (Exod 1:22), God intervenes in a way that subverts this injustice by ensuring Moses is protected, even in Pharaoh's household (Exod 2:5-6). This reflects God's commitment to protecting the oppressed and raising up leaders who will pursue justice. This section encourages us to trust in God's plan for justice, even when the systems of the world seem overwhelmingly unjust. It calls believers to engage in the pursuit of justice by standing against the political and social oppression of God's people, much like Moses's parents did by protecting him. Grounded in God's righteousness, believers today are called to advocate for liberty, justice, and the protection of life, reflecting the values of the coming kingdom of God (cf. Mic 6:8).

Spiritual Warfare

In Exod 2:1-8, Moses's family faces both spiritual and moral challenges. The decision to protect their son and defy Pharaoh's command (Exod 2:2-3) is an act of spiritual resistance against evil. This story demonstrates how spiritual warfare often involves protecting and preserving life, even in the face of unjust human laws. The spiritual courage required to protect Moses is a model of moral integrity and trust in God's protection.

Application Today: This passage equips us to stand firm in the face of moral and spiritual challenges, especially when society's laws or norms contradict God's commands. In our own lives, we are called to act with moral integrity, standing against evil and trusting that God will guide and protect us as we seek to live out his purposes. The courage displayed by Moses's family encourages believers to confront spiritual and moral challenges with faith and resilience (cf. Eph 6:12–13).

Questions for Reflection and Discussion

1. Jochebed had to trust God with her son's life by placing him in the basket (Exod 2:3). What situations in your life require you to trust in God's providence, even when the outcome is uncertain (cf. Phil 4:6–7)?

2. How do Jochebed's and Pharaoh's daughter's actions demonstrate courage in the face of fear and uncertainty (Exod 2:3–6)? How can we show similar courage in today's world when standing up for what is right (cf. 2 Tim 1:7)?

3. Despite Moses's vulnerability as an infant, God protected him through the actions of multiple women (Exod 2:4–6). How does this passage encourage us to see God's hand of protection even in situations where we feel powerless?

4. Jochebed and Pharaoh's daughter both resist Pharaoh's decree to kill the Hebrew boys (Exod 2:3, 6). In what ways can we, like them, stand up against injustice or evil in today's world (cf. Eph 6:12)?

Exodus 2:11-25

Context and Analysis

Exodus 2:11-25 takes place while the Israelites are still enslaved in Egypt. Moses, although raised in Pharaoh's household (Exod 2:10), is aware of his Hebrew identity. The passage covers a pivotal moment in Moses's life where he begins to see the injustice faced by his people, leading him to flee Egypt. The Egyptians' oppression of the Israelites is intense, creating a backdrop of suffering and conflict (Exod 1:13-14; 2:11). Moses responds to the mistreatment of a fellow Hebrew by killing an Egyptian (Exod 2:11-12). Fear of Pharaoh's wrath forces Moses to flee to Midian (Exod 2:15), where he helps protect the daughters of the priest of Midian at a well (Exod 2:17). This shows Moses's shift from acting impulsively to stepping into a more protective, peacekeeping role. The phrase "looked this way and that" (Exod 2:12) shows Moses's internal fear and uncertainty before acting, suggesting that his actions were motivated by human impulse rather than divine instruction. Water appears as a setting again, as Moses meets his future family by a well, a recurring symbol of provision in the Bible (Exod 2:15-17; cf. Gen 24:13).

Spiritual Insights: Basic Anxiety

Moses's anxiety is evident as he flees Egypt after realizing that his actions have been discovered (Exod 2:14-15). He experiences fear and helplessness, unsure of his future and identity as both a Hebrew and an Egyptian. Moses's initial coping strategy is self-expansion—he seeks to assert control by taking matters into his own hands when he kills the Egyptian (Exod 2:12). Later, he experiences self-resignation, withdrawing to Midian to escape his fear of Pharaoh (Exod 2:15). This withdrawal reflects his uncertainty about his future and his place in God's plan. At this stage, Moses is still trusting in his own strength and decision making, rather than seeking God's direction. His actions are shaped by fear and impulse rather than faith in God's timing and plan.

Problems and Dilemmas

Moses faces a moral dilemma in witnessing the mistreatment of his people and feeling compelled to intervene (Exod 2:11–12). However, his choice to kill the Egyptian raises questions about justice, control, and appropriate means of intervention. His flight from Egypt reflects an inner conflict between his role as a Hebrew and his upbringing in Pharaoh's household. Moses likely saw himself as a deliverer for his people, but his rash actions reveal his weakness and humanity. His flight to Midian highlights the contrast between his idealized role and his real self, who is still unsure of his calling and driven by fear (Exod 2:15). This passage raises questions about leadership and obedience. Moses's actions reflect the tension between standing against injustice and waiting for God's timing. The inner conflict he experiences about his identity and role as a leader becomes clearer as he transitions from Egypt to Midian.

Themes and Obligations

Moses's vulnerability is evident as he flees from Pharaoh's wrath (Exod 2:15). Yet, God's protection is subtly seen in his successful journey to Midian and the hospitality he finds with Reuel (Exod 2:18–21). This shows that even when Moses acts out of fear, God's providential care is still at work. The passage places an emphasis on justice and intervention. Moses tries to act on behalf of the oppressed Hebrews, but his violent response highlights the need for wisdom and patience in pursuing justice. The ethical challenge is balancing intervention with waiting on God's guidance. Moses's intent to defend his people is noble, but it is marred by impulsive actions and fear. His later intervention to help the daughters of the priest of Midian is a more peaceful and righteous form of protection (Exod 2:17).

Reflections and Application

Moses's fear of failure and his decision to flee after his violent act (Exod 2:15) resonate with many modern struggles. This passage speaks to those who face challenges and fear of inadequacy, reminding us that God is at work even when we feel lost or afraid (cf. 2 Cor 12:9). Moses's attempt to save his people on his own terms reflects how we sometimes set unattainable expectations for ourselves, acting without God's guidance. This passage encourages us to rely on God's wisdom rather than our own impulsive actions (cf. Prov 3:5-6). Moses's growth from a reactive leader to a more thoughtful protector in Midian reflects the journey many leaders face in learning to act with patience and discernment. This passage invites leaders to consider how they balance righteous anger with measured action.

God's Sovereignty and Providence

Although God is not explicitly mentioned in these verses, his providence is evident. Moses is preserved through his exile in Midian, and his encounter with Reuel's family sets the stage for his future calling (Exod 2:15-22). God's plan is unfolding, even through Moses's mistakes and fears. Moses's actions show a failure to fully recognize God's timing and authority. He acts on his own initiative rather than waiting for God's direction, but God's grace continues to work in Moses's life, preparing him for future leadership.

Covenant Relationship and Faithfulness

God's faithfulness to his covenant people is reflected in his hearing of their cries (Exod 2:23-24). Even though Moses flees, God remembers his covenant with Abraham, Isaac, and Jacob, and his plan for deliverance continues to unfold (Exod 2:24-25). God's faithfulness in this chapter encourages believers to trust that, despite human failure or delay, his promises endure. Moses's fear and flight do not derail God's plan for Israel's redemption (cf. Rom 8:28).

Human Vocation and Cultural Mandate

Moses's attempt to defend the Hebrew slave reflects a sense of vocation, but his methods show a lack of maturity in leadership (Exod 2:12). His time in Midian allows him to develop as a shepherd, preparing him for future leadership of God's people (cf. Exod 3:1). This section emphasizes the importance of acting in accordance with God's timing and serving others, not out of impulse, but with wisdom and patience.

Common Grace and Resistance to Evil

Moses's confrontation with the Egyptian (Exod 2:11–12) reflects the ongoing struggle between the oppressed and the oppressor. Moses's actions highlight the complexity of responding to evil, as his initial act of violence leads to further conflict. Moses's failed attempt to deliver justice through violence contrasts with his later, more peaceful intervention at the well (Exod 2:17). This passage challenges us to resist evil in ways that align with God's principles of justice and peace.

God's Grace and Redemptive History

Despite Moses's flawed attempt at deliverance, God's grace remains evident. Moses's exile becomes part of his preparation for future leadership, showing how God's redemptive purposes work through human weakness (Exod 2:15–22; cf. 2 Cor 12:9–10). This section invites us to trust that God is working through the challenges and mistakes in our lives to bring about his redemptive plan.

Cultural Mandate and Kingdom Work

Exodus 2:11–15 reflects the brokenness of the world and the need for justice and stewardship of human relationships. The cultural mandate given to humanity is to cultivate and steward all of creation, including social relationships, justice, and human dignity. Moses, seeing the injustice of an Egyptian beating a Hebrew, takes action but in a misguided way, revealing the tension between the desire for justice and the correct means of achieving it (Exod 2:11–12).

Application Today: This passage informs our role as agents of renewal by reminding us that while the impulse to address injustice is right, our actions must align with God's wisdom and righteousness. We are called to cultivate justice, peace, and order in the world, knowing that God is the ultimate restorer of all things. Our work and engagement should reflect this vision, participating in God's mission to renew creation while exercising patience and dependence on him in the process (Rom 12:19).

Social Mandate and Family Life

This passage hints at the importance of the broader family of God's covenant people. Moses's identification with his fellow Israelites shows the social solidarity within God's people. However, his impulsive action results in social breakdown, forcing him to flee to Midian and alienating him from both the Egyptians and his own people (Exod 2:13-15). The fracture of these relationships shows the importance of upholding God's order in social and family life.

Application Today: The social mandate is to live in covenantal community where family and society reflect God's order and purpose. Moses's actions and their consequences reveal the importance of acting justly, not through force or violence, but through God's wisdom and patience. Families and communities today are called to foster godliness, solidarity, and mutual support, recognizing their role in advancing God's purposes in a broken world (Eph 4:1-3). The passage also shows how misguided actions can break social and familial bonds, reminding us to seek God's wisdom in our dealings with others.

Liberty, Justice, and God's Kingdom

Exodus 2:11-15 reveals God's deep concern for justice, as Moses is stirred by the mistreatment of the Hebrew by the Egyptian. Moses's act of killing the Egyptian (Exod 2:12) reflects a premature attempt to achieve justice outside of God's timing and wisdom. This passage demonstrates that true justice is grounded in God's righteousness, not human effort or violent retribution.

Application Today: The pursuit of justice today must be grounded in God's character and law, not in human ideals of power or control. Moses's failure shows that when we pursue justice in our own strength, it can lead to further harm or disarray. We are called to engage in the pursuit of political, social, and economic liberty, but in a way that reflects the coming kingdom of God, which is marked by righteousness, peace, and humility (Isa 9:7). This passage calls us to wait on God's timing and direction, trusting that he will bring about justice in his way (Mic 6:8).

Spiritual Warfare

Exodus 2:11-15 presents Moses with a spiritual and moral challenge—how to respond to the injustice he witnesses. His immediate response, though well intentioned, lacks moral integrity as it is carried out through violence and secrecy (Exod 2:12). This decision results in Moses becoming a fugitive, revealing the consequences of responding to moral challenges without seeking God's guidance.

Application Today: In the battle for justice and righteousness, believers face similar spiritual and moral challenges. This passage encourages us to resist the temptation to act out of anger or human strength when confronted with evil. Instead, we must rely on God's guidance, maintaining moral integrity and trusting in his justice (Eph 6:12–13). Moses's journey reminds us that life is a battleground where we must navigate spiritual warfare with wisdom, prayer, and trust in God's ultimate plan for his people and kingdom.

Questions for Reflection and Discussion

1. Like Moses, we often feel compelled to act when we see injustice (Exod 2:11–12). How can we ensure that our actions reflect God's wisdom and timing rather than impulsive reactions (cf. Jas 1:19–20)?

2. Moses flees Egypt in fear after his initial attempt to deliver his people fails (Exod 2:14–15). How does this passage help us navigate our own failures and trust that God can still use us despite our mistakes (cf. 2 Cor 12:9)?

3. Though Moses fled in fear, God was still at work preparing him for his future role (Exod 2:15–22). Can you identify times in your life when God's providence was at work, even when you felt lost or exiled?

4. Moses's violent response to oppression contrasts with his later peaceful intervention at the well (Exod 2:17). How does this passage challenge us to consider the ways we respond to evil and injustice in today's world (cf. Eph 6:12–13)?

Exodus 3

Context and Analysis

At the time of Exod 3, the Israelites have been enslaved in Egypt for many years (Exod 1:11–14). Moses, who fled from Egypt after killing an Egyptian, has been living in Midian for approximately forty years (Exod 2:15–23). In this chapter, God calls Moses through the burning bush to return to Egypt and lead his people out of slavery. The cultural and historical context reveals the oppression of the Israelites, which sets the stage for God's divine intervention (Exod 3:7–9). Moses responds to God's call with fear and reluctance, expressing self-doubt (Exod 3:11, 13). God reassures Moses, affirming his divine authority and promising his presence (Exod 3:12, 14). God's declaration of "I Am Who I Am" (Exod 3:14) emphasizes his eternal existence and sovereignty, which contrasts with Moses's vulnerability and fear. The burning bush (Exod 3:2) is a key symbol, representing God's holiness and his presence with Israel. Fire often symbolizes divine presence and purification (cf. Exod 19:18; Heb 12:29). The theme of seeing and hearing is repeated as God declares that he has "seen the misery" and "heard the cries" of his people (Exod 3:7), demonstrating his concern and care. This seeing and hearing sets the God of Israel apart from the impotence of false gods and idols, which do not exist and are incapable of acting in time and space. They can neither see nor hear.

Spiritual Insights: Basic Anxiety

Moses experiences deep anxiety and insecurity when God calls him to confront Pharaoh and lead the Israelites (Exod 3:11). He feels inadequate and uncertain of his ability to fulfill this task. Moses exhibits self-resignation, as he questions God, "Who am I that I should go to Pharaoh?" (Exod 3:11). His lack of confidence in his own abilities causes him to retreat emotionally, relying on excuses rather than trust in God. Moses initially trusts in his own inadequacy, but God directs Moses to trust in his divine presence: "I will be with you" (Exod 3:12). The shift from relying on self to relying on God is crucial for Moses's transformation as a leader.

Problems and Dilemmas

Moses is faced with the dilemma of obeying God's command to return to Egypt, where he fled from after killing an Egyptian (Exod 2:15). His fear of returning reflects a deep internal conflict between his past actions and his calling to be the leader of the Israelites. Moses wrestles with his identity—he sees himself as unworthy and incapable, yet God sees him as his chosen instrument to deliver Israel. This contrast between Moses's real self and the leader God is shaping him to become is a recurring theme (Exod 3:11–12). Moses's reluctance to accept God's call reveals deeper questions about obedience, faith, and leadership. His self-doubt raises the issue of trusting in God's power versus relying on human capability (Exod 3:11, 13).

Themes and Obligations

The burning bush represents God's protective presence amidst human vulnerability. Moses is commanded to remove his sandals because he is on holy ground (Exod 3:5), reminding him of the sacredness and power of God. Despite Moses's vulnerability, God's promise of presence assures his protection (Exod 3:12). God places a significant responsibility on Moses, calling him to lead his people out of bondage (Exod 3:10). This call to justice challenges Moses—and, by extension, believers—to step beyond fear and self-interest to serve the community and fulfill God's will. Moses's fear initially hinders him from accepting the noble goal of liberating the Israelites. However, God's reassurance enables Moses to move past his fear and focus on the higher purpose of delivering God's people (Exod 3:11–14).

Reflections and Application

Like Moses, many people today struggle with insecurity and fear of failure when faced with a daunting task. God's reassurance to Moses—"I will be with you"—serves as a reminder that we do not face challenges alone (Exod

3:12; cf. Matt 28:20). Moses initially sets unattainable expectations for himself, believing he needs to possess all the skills to accomplish God's mission. This passage reminds us that faithfulness, rather than perfection, is what God requires (cf. 1 Cor 1:26–27).

Application Today: In leadership, community work, or personal challenges, God's call to Moses invites us to respond to injustices around us with courage, trusting that God will equip us for his purposes. Whether facing oppression, family struggles, or societal issues, the promise of God's presence remains central.

God's Sovereignty and Providence

God's declaration of his name, "I AM WHO I AM" (Exod 3:14), reveals his eternal and unchanging nature. This demonstrates that God's plan for Israel's deliverance is rooted in his sovereign will and power, beyond human comprehension or ability. Moses is initially reluctant to embrace his leadership role because he is focused on his own limitations. God's command challenges Moses to recognize his authority, power, and faithfulness in all areas of life and leadership (Exod 3:14–15).

Covenant Relationship and Faithfulness

God's call to Moses is framed in the context of his covenant with Abraham, Isaac, and Jacob (Exod 3:6, 15–16). God's faithfulness to his people extends through generations, and Moses's mission is a continuation of this covenant promise. The burning bush encounter reflects God's unwavering commitment to his covenant. God's assurance that he has seen the suffering of his people (Exod 3:7–9) serves as a reminder of his faithfulness and commitment to justice. This should encourage believers to remain faithful to their responsibilities in the church and community, trusting in God's presence.

Human Vocation and Cultural Mandate

Moses is given the monumental responsibility of leading the Israelites out of Egypt (Exod 3:10). His calling reflects the broader call of God's people to stand for justice, care for others, and cultivate God's creation in alignment with his will. This section highlights that God's people are called to both spiritual and practical work—standing against oppression while leading others toward God's purposes (cf. Matt 20:26–28).

Common Grace and Resistance to Evil

Pharaoh represents the forces of evil and oppression, while God's calling of Moses embodies the beginning of Israel's liberation. God's grace is evident in his commitment to intervene on behalf of his people (Exod 3:9–10). God's charge to Moses to confront Pharaoh shows that resisting evil is part of the vocation of God's people. This is not done in human strength but through the power and authority of God (cf. Eph 6:12–13).

God's Grace and Redemptive History

The calling of Moses is part of the larger story of redemption, which culminates in Christ. God's intervention through Moses foreshadows the ultimate deliverance that Jesus brings (cf. John 8:58, where Jesus identifies himself as "I Am"). Moses's call to lead Israel out of slavery invites us to reflect on how we are called to participate in God's redemptive work in our communities. This includes addressing injustice, serving others, and embodying God's grace.

Cultural Mandate and Kingdom Work

In Exod 3, God's call to Moses from the burning bush is deeply rooted in the cultural mandate to steward and cultivate creation. God reveals himself as the creator and sustainer of all things, calling Moses to lead his people out of Egypt and restore them to their land—a task that directly involves the care and stewardship of his people and their land (Exod 3:8). The cultural mandate, given in Gen 1:28, involves humanity's role in cultivating, governing, and stewarding the world under God's authority. Moses's leadership is part of God's broader plan for his people to flourish in the promised land, where they can fulfill their calling to be a blessing to all nations (cf. Gen 12:2–3).

Application Today: Today, believers are called to engage in their work and communities as agents of God's kingdom renewal, participating in the restoration of all things through faithfulness to God's design for creation. Just as Moses was called to lead the people out of bondage, we are called to work toward the restoration of God's created order, advancing his kingdom in every sphere of life—family, work, culture, and society. This includes cultivating environments of justice, peace, and flourishing that reflect God's rule (cf. Col 3:23–24).

Social Mandate and Family Life

Exodus 3 addresses the social and familial dynamics of God's covenant people by calling Moses to lead them out of Egypt and back into the land God had promised to their ancestors (Exod 3:6–8). The social mandate is inherently tied to the well-being of God's people, particularly their families and communities. God is not only delivering them from physical slavery but also restoring their identity as his chosen people, a community that is called to live in covenant faithfulness.

Application Today: This section highlights the importance of godly leadership in preserving and advancing the social and family life of God's people. Families are foundational in passing on the covenantal promises of God, and communities of faith are essential in reflecting the kingdom of God. Our responsibility today is to strengthen families and communities so that they are aligned with God's purposes, fostering environments where God's word is central and his covenant is upheld. In doing so, we advance God's purposes for the world (cf. Deut 6:6–9).

Liberty, Justice, and God's Kingdom

Exodus 3 reveals God's deep concern for justice and liberation. God says, "I have indeed seen the misery of my people in Egypt. I have heard them crying out because of their slave drivers, and I am concerned about their suffering" (Exod 3:7). God's response to the oppression of his people demonstrates his commitment to justice and freedom, especially for those suffering under political and economic bondage. The liberation of the Israelites is part of God's larger plan to establish a people who reflect his righteousness and justice. This section calls us to pursue justice in our own societies by reflecting God's heart for the oppressed and marginalized. Just as Moses was called to confront Pharaoh and lead the people out of slavery, we are called to engage in the pursuit of liberty and justice that reflects God's kingdom values. This pursuit should be grounded in God's righteousness and his law, leading to the protection of human dignity, the defense of the oppressed, and the promotion of freedom that glorifies God (cf. Mic 6:8).

Spiritual Warfare

In Exod 3, Moses is faced with significant spiritual and moral challenges. He feels inadequate to fulfill the task God has set before him, expressing doubts about his ability to confront Pharaoh and lead the Israelites (Exod

3:11–13). This reflects the ongoing spiritual battle between fear and faith. God's response to Moses's fear is to reassure him of his divine presence: "I will be with you" (Exod 3:12), emphasizing that victory comes through reliance on God, not human strength.

Application Today: The spiritual warfare in this passage points to the need for moral integrity and trust in God's provision when facing challenges in our own lives. Believers are often called to confront difficult situations where they may feel inadequate, but God's promise to be with his people reminds us that the battle belongs to him. Standing firm in the face of moral and spiritual challenges requires courage, faith, and reliance on God's word and his presence. As we engage in spiritual warfare, we are equipped to live with integrity, knowing that our strength comes from God alone (cf. Eph 6:10–13).

Questions for Reflection and Discussion

1. Moses doubted his ability to fulfill God's call due to his insecurity (Exod 3:11). How can you trust God more fully when faced with your own inadequacies? What steps of faith can you take when God calls you to challenging tasks in your personal life or ministry (cf. Phil 4:13)?

2. God hears the cries of his people and commissions Moses to bring justice (Exod 3:7–10). How are we, as God's people today, called to address injustice in our communities? What are practical ways you can serve those who are oppressed or in need (cf. Matt 25:35–40)?

3. Moses hesitates and makes excuses for why he cannot lead (Exod 3:13). In what areas of your life do you make excuses instead of stepping into God's calling? How can you move from fear to trust in God's provision for his mission (cf. 2 Tim 1:7)?

4. God assures Moses that his presence will go with him (Exod 3:12). How can recognizing God's presence transform the way you lead or serve in your family, church, or community? How does this affect your role in bringing about positive change in society?

Exodus 4:1-17

Context and Analysis

In Exod 4:1–17, Moses continues his dialogue with God at the burning bush. After God calls Moses to lead the Israelites out of Egypt (Exod 3), Moses expresses doubts and concerns about his ability to fulfill this role. The Israelites are still enslaved, and Pharaoh's oppression has intensified. This context of oppression and suffering clarifies the challenges Moses will face in leading the Israelites. God responds to Moses's doubts by providing signs and assurances, equipping him for the task. Moses is hesitant and expresses fear that the Israelites will not believe that God has sent him (Exod 4:1). God provides Moses with signs, such as the staff turning into a snake (Exod 4:3) and his hand becoming leprous (Exod 4:6), to show God's divine power and reassure him. Moses still expresses insecurity about his speaking abilities (Exod 4:10), but God promises to be with him and appoints Aaron as his spokesperson (Exod 4:14–16). The use of Moses's staff as a symbol of God's power (Exod 4:2–4) and the signs of healing (leprous hand) demonstrate that God's divine intervention will guide and protect Moses. The phrase "I will be with you" (Exod 4:12, 15) emphasizes God's promise of presence and guidance, underscoring the theme of divine provision.

Spiritual Insights: Basic Anxiety

Moses feels insecure and anxious about his ability to lead the Israelites (Exod 4:1, 10). His fear of failure and rejection by both the Israelites and Pharaoh dominates his response to God's call. Moses exhibits self-effacing behavior, expressing feelings of inadequacy and a lack of confidence in his speaking abilities (Exod 4:10). He repeatedly tries to avoid the task by focusing on his perceived limitations. Moses initially trusts in his own limitations rather than in God's promise and power. God, however, redirects Moses to trust in his divine provision, assuring him that he will equip and empower him (Exod 4:11–12). This reflects the broader spiritual lesson of moving from self-reliance to reliance on God.

Problems and Dilemmas

Moses faces a spiritual dilemma of faith and obedience. He struggles with trusting God's plan, fearing that his limitations will prevent him from successfully leading the Israelites (Exod 4:1, 10). This dilemma reflects a deeper conflict between human insecurity and divine calling. Moses's view of himself is shaped by his perceived weaknesses (Exod 4:10). He sees himself as inadequate, yet God calls him to a higher role, showing that divine leadership is not based on human perfection but on God's power. This passage raises questions about obedience to God's call despite fear. Moses's hesitation reveals the tension between personal inadequacy and the faith required to step into God's plans. God's solution—appointing Aaron as Moses's spokesperson (Exod 4:14–16)—shows how God accommodates human weakness while still advancing his purposes.

Themes and Obligations

God's response to Moses's insecurity is a promise of his protection and guidance (Exod 4:12). Despite Moses's vulnerability, God assures him that his power will be enough to accomplish the task. The signs provided (staff turning into a snake, leprous hand) demonstrate God's authority over both life and death. Moses is given the responsibility to lead God's people out of slavery, a task that comes with moral and ethical implications. His initial reluctance highlights the struggle of accepting difficult responsibilities, but God's persistence demonstrates that serving others and fulfilling God's plan is a higher moral calling. Moses's fear nearly hinders him from pursuing the noble goal of delivering the Israelites (Exod 4:13). However, God's reassurance and provision enable Moses to step into his role, showing that noble pursuits often require overcoming personal fears.

Reflections and Application

Many individuals today struggle with feelings of inadequacy, similar to Moses's fears about his speaking abilities (Exod 4:10). God's response—that he will give Moses the words to speak (Exod 4:12)—reminds us that we can trust in God's equipping power when we feel insufficient for a task. Moses's doubts reflect the unrealistic expectation that he needs to be perfect in order to fulfill God's mission. This passage encourages us to reject the pursuit of perfection and instead embrace faithful obedience, trusting that God's power is made perfect in our weakness (cf. 2 Cor 12:9). Leadership in modern communities often requires stepping into roles we feel unprepared for. Like Moses, we may doubt our abilities, but God calls us to trust in his provision. Whether leading in church, family, or society, the message of this passage is to rely on God's strength rather than our own.

God's Sovereignty and Providence

This passage demonstrates God's sovereignty in choosing and equipping his leaders. Despite Moses's resistance, God has a plan for delivering Israel, and he reassures Moses that his purposes will prevail (Exod 4:12). The signs given to Moses show that God is in control of the situation, including nature and health (Exod 4:2–9). Moses's reluctance to obey reveals a struggle to fully recognize God's authority. God challenges Moses to trust in his power and presence, showing that leadership is not based on human strength but on submission to divine authority (Exod 4:11–12).

Covenant Relationship and Faithfulness

God's promise to be with Moses and guide him reflects his covenant faithfulness to Israel. God is preparing Moses to fulfill his covenant promises to Abraham, Isaac, and Jacob by delivering Israel from slavery (Exod 4:5). Moses's mission is directly connected to the unfolding of God's redemptive plan. God's persistent encouragement of Moses, despite his reluctance, reminds us of God's faithfulness even when we are hesitant. This passage encourages us to be faithful in our responsibilities to God, trusting that he will equip us for the tasks he has called us to.

Human Vocation and Cultural Mandate

Moses is called to lead the Israelites, a task that involves both spiritual and practical leadership. His vocation aligns with God's broader cultural mandate to care for his people and lead them out of bondage (Exod 4:10; cf. Gen 1:28). God's call to Moses highlights the importance of serving others in alignment with his purposes. Moses's leadership is part of God's mission to cultivate justice and liberation for his people.

Common Grace and Resistance to Evil

The tension between Pharaoh's oppressive regime and God's plan for liberation is central to this passage. Moses is chosen to confront evil (represented by Pharaoh) and bring freedom to the Israelites. God's power, demonstrated through the signs, foreshadows the ultimate defeat of evil forces (Exod 4:2–9). Moses's mission to confront Pharaoh reflects the call to resist evil and injustice. This passage challenges believers to trust in God's power when standing against oppressive systems, knowing that God equips us for the fight (cf. Eph 6:10–13).

God's Grace and Redemptive History

God's choice of Moses, despite his reluctance and fears, highlights his grace in using imperfect people for his redemptive purposes. Moses's mission foreshadows the greater deliverance that will come through Christ, the ultimate deliverer (cf. Luke 4:18–19). This passage invites believers to participate in God's redemptive work by confronting injustice, trusting that God's grace empowers us to accomplish his purposes. Moses's story reminds us that God's grace covers our weaknesses and insecurities.

Cultural Mandate and Kingdom Work

In Exod 4:1–17, the cultural mandate to steward creation is reflected in God's call to Moses to lead Israel out of Egypt. Moses is called to cultivate the freedom of God's people and guide them to the promised land where they can flourish as a nation. God equips Moses with signs (Exod 4:2–9) to demonstrate his authority and power, emphasizing the human responsibility to act as God's agents of renewal in creation. The staff that becomes a snake and Moses's hand turning leprous serve as signs that creation is under God's dominion, and that human leadership is part of God's plan for cultivating his kingdom.

Application Today: This passage calls believers today to recognize their role in stewarding both creation and societal structures. Just as Moses was called to bring order and freedom to a chaotic, enslaved people, we are called to be agents of restoration in our communities, workplaces, and families. Our work, whether in secular or church contexts, participates in God's broader mission to restore all things to their proper order, reflecting his reign in every area of life (cf. Col 3:23-24).

Social Mandate and Family Life

Exodus 4:1-17 reveals the importance of community and family in fulfilling God's purposes. Although Moses is hesitant and insecure about his ability to lead (Exod 4:10), God provides Aaron, his brother, to assist him (Exod 4:14-16). This reflects the significance of family and communal support in carrying out God's mission. Moses's eventual return to his family in Egypt will play a crucial role in uniting the Israelites and leading them to freedom.

Application Today: This section highlights the importance of family and community dynamics in advancing God's purposes. Families and communities are to work together in obedience to God's call, reflecting his order and authority. In today's context, the family is essential for nurturing faith and preparing individuals to serve in God's kingdom. The church, as a covenant community, plays a vital role in supporting individuals as they pursue their God-given callings. The mutual dependence and collaboration between Moses and Aaron remind us that God's purposes are often accomplished through communal efforts, not individualism (cf. 1 Cor 12:12-26).

Liberty, Justice, and God's Kingdom

God's call to Moses to deliver the Israelites from oppression reveals his deep concern for justice. In Exod 4:1-17, God equips Moses with signs to demonstrate his power over Pharaoh and the unjust Egyptian system. The focus on political liberty is central to this passage as God's ultimate goal is the liberation of his people from slavery. This reflects God's concern not only for spiritual salvation but also for political and social freedom.

Application Today: This passage calls believers to pursue justice in a way that reflects the coming kingdom of God. Just as God sent Moses to confront Pharaoh's injustice, we are called to engage in the pursuit of justice, whether it is political, economic, or social. However, this justice must be grounded in God's righteousness, not human ideals of power or coercion. The signs given to Moses—such as turning the staff into a snake—reveal that God's justice operates through his sovereign power, not human force (cf. Mic 6:8). Our pursuit of justice today should therefore reflect God's values of righteousness, humility, and dependence on his will.

Spiritual Warfare

In Exod 4:1–17, Moses faces significant spiritual and moral challenges as he doubts his own ability to lead. His insecurity about his speaking abilities (Exod 4:10) reflects an internal spiritual battle. God responds with reassurance, reminding Moses that it is God who gives humans their abilities and that he will equip Moses for the task (Exod 4:11–12). This passage reflects the tension between human weakness and divine calling, showing that spiritual warfare often involves confronting our own doubts and insecurities.

Application Today: The spiritual and moral challenges faced by Moses are ones that believers continue to face today. When called to difficult tasks, many experience feelings of inadequacy or fear. However, this passage encourages believers to trust in God's sovereignty and provision. The signs that God gives to Moses serve as a reminder that God is with his people, empowering them to fulfill their calling. In our own lives, we are called to stand firm in the face of spiritual warfare, relying on God's strength rather than our own abilities (cf. Eph 6:10–13). Moral integrity requires obedience to God's call, even when we feel inadequate, trusting that he will provide the means to accomplish his purposes.

Questions for Reflection and Discussion

1. Like Moses, we often feel inadequate for the tasks God calls us to (Exod 4:10). How can you trust in God's provision and strength when you feel unqualified for a role or responsibility? What steps of faith can you take when facing insecurity (cf. Phil 4:13)?

2. Moses's fear nearly prevented him from stepping into his calling (Exod 4:13). How does this passage challenge you to serve your community, even when you feel afraid or unsure of your abilities? What role does faith play in overcoming fear in leadership?

3. Moses felt inadequate due to his speaking ability (Exod 4:10), but God provided Aaron to help. How can recognizing your weaknesses

help you depend more on God's strength and the support of others? How does this apply to working in community with others for God's purposes (cf. 2 Cor 12:9)?

4. Moses is called to confront the oppression of Pharaoh (Exod 4:2–5). In what ways are you called to stand against injustice in your community or society? How does this passage encourage you to trust in God's power when confronting difficult situations or oppressive systems (cf. Eph 6:10–13)?

Exodus 4:18–31

Context and Analysis

In Exod 4:18–31, Moses finally accepts God's call and begins his journey back to Egypt to fulfill his mission to deliver the Israelites from slavery. He seeks permission from his father-in-law, Jethro, to return to Egypt (Exod 4:18). This section covers key moments, including Moses's reunion with Aaron and the critical intervention by his wife, Zipporah, in circumcising their son to prevent God's judgment (Exod 4:24–26). The tension between God's deliverance of Israel and the importance of covenant obedience is underscored. Moses acts obediently by returning to Egypt, but the incident where the Lord seeks to kill him (Exod 4:24) reveals a failure to circumcise his son, a key covenant requirement (cf. Gen 17:10–14). Zipporah's quick action in circumcising their son demonstrates the importance of obedience to God's covenant. Aaron, who meets Moses, plays a supportive role as the two begin their mission together (Exod 4:27–31). The phrase "the Lord said" occurs several times (Exod 4:19, 21), indicating divine authority over the events. The act of circumcision symbolizes the covenant between God and his people (Exod 4:25), representing the importance of obedience to God's commands in the unfolding of his plans.

Spiritual Insights: Basic Anxiety

Moses might have felt anxiety and fear about returning to Egypt, knowing the potential dangers. His failure to circumcise his son also suggests a deeper spiritual negligence that creates tension in his relationship with God. The passage indicates that Zipporah's intervention in circumcising their son relieved this fear of divine judgment (Exod 4:24–26). Moses seeks permission from Jethro, which shows a respectful and careful approach to leaving Midian (Exod 4:18). However, his delay in circumcising his son suggests self-resignation—perhaps hoping to avoid confronting the full responsibilities of the covenant. Zipporah takes decisive action to fulfill the covenant requirement (Exod 4:25). The near-death encounter (Exod 4:24) reveals that while Moses is obeying God outwardly, he has neglected an essential part of the covenant. Trusting God involves complete obedience, not partial compliance. Zipporah's actions show an immediate return to trust in God's command.

Problems and Dilemmas

The passage presents a spiritual dilemma regarding obedience to God's covenant. Moses had been chosen by God for a mission, but his failure to circumcise his son nearly resulted in divine punishment (Exod 4:24). This raises questions about the balance between God's grace and the necessity of covenant faithfulness. Moses's real self is revealed in his incomplete obedience. He is shown to be imperfect, yet God still chooses him. Zipporah's intervention underscores the importance of obedience, regardless of Moses's perceived leadership role. The deeper conflict is the tension between God's promise of deliverance and the requirement for his people to obey the covenant. Even the leader chosen to bring deliverance must fully adhere to God's commands. This moment clarifies that leadership in God's kingdom involves both faithfulness and action.

Themes and Obligations

Moses, despite being God's chosen instrument, is vulnerable to God's judgment for failing to meet covenant requirements (Exod 4:24). This underscores that divine protection is accompanied by obligations to follow God's commands. Moses is responsible for leading the Israelites, but this leadership must be rooted in full covenant obedience. Zipporah's quick action in circumcising their son (Exod 4:25) highlights the ethical responsibility of fulfilling God's commands as part of a leader's role. Moses's mission to liberate the Israelites is noble, but his failure to complete the circumcision reveals a tension between his public mission and private obedience. His pursuit of the goal of liberation requires aligning his family life with God's covenantal demands (Exod 4:24–26).

Reflections and Application

Like Moses, leaders today may face moments of insecurity, fear, and failure to fully obey God's commands. The passage reminds us that while God may call us to great things, complete obedience in the small details of life is equally important (cf. Luke 16:10). Moses's near-death encounter serves as a reminder that leadership and public service must be accompanied by private faithfulness. God calls his people to live in obedience and faithfulness to the covenant (cf. Rom 2:28-29).

Application Today: This passage speaks to modern leaders and communities who may seek to pursue justice and liberation but neglect spiritual and covenantal responsibilities. It reminds us that social action must be accompanied by a faithful commitment to God's commands.

God's Sovereignty and Providence

The passage demonstrates God's sovereignty in shaping the events of Moses's life. Even as Moses begins his mission, God's providence is clear in directing him and Aaron, and in ensuring that Moses's family adheres to the covenant (Exod 4:24-25, 27). God's plan will not be thwarted, but it requires faithful obedience. Moses's near-death experience reminds him—and us—of the seriousness of God's commands. Leading God's people requires recognizing his authority in all aspects of life, not just public service (Exod 4:24).

Covenant Relationship and Faithfulness

The incident of circumcision (Exod 4:24-26) directly connects to the covenant God made with Abraham (Gen 17:10-14). Even as Moses is called to lead Israel, his family must also align with this covenant. Faithfulness to the covenant is required for both leader and community. Moses's experience, combined with Zipporah's actions, teaches us that faithfulness to God's covenant may involve hard decisions but is critical for receiving God's continued blessing and protection (Exod 4:25).

Human Vocation and Cultural Mandate

Moses is stepping fully into his vocation as the leader and deliverer of Israel, but this vocation requires aligning both his personal life and public mission with God's commands (Exod 4:18, 25). His calling involves leading Israel while ensuring his family life reflects God's covenant. As Moses begins his mission, the importance of stewardship over family and community becomes clear. Leaders are called to ensure that both their private and public lives reflect God's covenantal values.

Common Grace and Resistance to Evil

God's plan to liberate Israel from Egyptian oppression is taking shape, but even Moses faces spiritual challenges along the way. His near-death experience serves as a reminder of the seriousness of covenant obedience, even as he prepares to confront the evil of Pharaoh's regime (Exod 4:24-26). Moses's mission to deliver Israel is part of God's broader plan to resist evil and oppression. This passage challenges us to remember that personal and family obedience to God's commands is essential when confronting broader societal injustices.

God's Grace and Redemptive History

God's grace is evident in his patience with Moses. Despite Moses's delay in circumcising his son, God's grace allows for Zipporah's intervention, ensuring that Moses can continue his mission. This incident foreshadows God's redemptive plan for his people, culminating in Christ's ultimate deliverance (cf. Col 2:11-12). The passage challenges believers to align their personal lives with God's redemptive work. Even as we pursue social justice or leadership, obedience to God's covenant is essential.

Cultural Mandate and Kingdom Work

In Exod 4:18-31, Moses begins to act on his divine calling to lead Israel out of bondage. He returns to Egypt with the explicit purpose of bringing God's people to a place where they can serve and worship him freely (Exod 4:22-23). This reflects the broader cultural mandate given in Genesis to steward and cultivate creation in a way that honors God. Moses is leading Israel toward a land where they can fulfill their covenantal responsibilities, live freely, and cultivate society in a manner aligned with God's commandments.

Application Today: Today, we are called to be agents of renewal in our work and communities, engaging in efforts that reflect God's kingdom purposes. Like Moses, our work should point toward God's ultimate plan for renewal, whether that is through faithful stewardship of the environment, cultivating justice in society, or advancing cultural and vocational initiatives that reflect God's order. This section encourages us to approach our daily tasks as part of God's larger mission to restore all things to himself (cf. Col 3:17).

Social Mandate and Family Life

Exodus 4:18–31 highlights the importance of family dynamics and the continuity of God's covenant through generations. Moses returns to Egypt with his family (Exod 4:20), and during the journey, there is a critical moment in which Zipporah circumcises their son (Exod 4:24–26). This act, though seemingly perplexing, emphasizes the importance of maintaining the covenantal sign given to Abraham and passing it down through family lines. The neglect of circumcision nearly results in God's wrath against Moses, but Zipporah's intervention restores the covenantal order within their family.

Application Today: This section teaches the importance of upholding God's covenant within the family structure. Parents have a responsibility to ensure that their children are raised within the covenant community, understanding their relationship to God and his commands. In today's world, this means prioritizing the spiritual formation of children, ensuring that they are taught God's word and guided in their faith journey. The family is essential for advancing God's purposes and passing down the faith through generations (cf. Deut 6:6–9).

Liberty, Justice, and God's Kingdom

Exodus 4:18–31 underscores God's commitment to justice and liberation. God commands Moses to tell Pharaoh, "Let my son go, so that he may worship me," referring to Israel as his "firstborn son" (Exod 4:22–23). This demonstrates God's protective and fatherly care for his people, and his determination to liberate them from unjust political and economic oppression. Moses's mission to confront Pharaoh is a clear pursuit of liberty and justice, grounded in God's righteous character.

Application Today: The chapter calls believers to be advocates of justice and freedom, especially in the face of oppressive systems. Just as God sent Moses to deliver Israel, we are called to stand for those who are politically, socially, or economically oppressed. However, our pursuit of justice must be grounded in God's righteousness and reflect the values of his coming kingdom. In standing for liberty, we point others toward the greater liberation that is found in Christ (cf. Luke 4:18–19).

Spiritual Warfare

Exodus 4:18–31 highlights the spiritual warfare that Moses faces as he obeys God's call. The encounter where God seeks to kill Moses (Exod 4:24–26) reveals the spiritual stakes of neglecting covenantal obligations. Moses is in a battle not only with Pharaoh but also within himself, as he wrestles with fear and doubt. The confrontation about circumcision also shows how seriously God views covenant faithfulness and the moral integrity required for those leading his people. This passage calls believers to maintain moral integrity and faithfulness to God's commands, even in the midst of spiritual warfare. We are often tempted to neglect certain areas of obedience, but God's expectations for holiness remain. The battle for faithfulness is real, and we must remain vigilant in our spiritual lives, guarding against complacency and disobedience. In facing spiritual and moral challenges, believers are called to stand firm in the strength that God provides, knowing that the battle belongs to the Lord (cf. Eph 6:10–18).

Questions for Reflection and Discussion

1. Moses's mission to lead the Israelites was nearly derailed by a failure in his personal life (Exod 4:24). How can we ensure that our personal and family lives are aligned with God's covenant as we pursue public or community service? What are practical steps for maintaining integrity in both private and public spheres?

2. Moses was called to liberate an entire nation, but the incident of circumcision showed the importance of private obedience (Exod 4:25). How can we, as leaders in our communities or families, balance the responsibilities of public leadership with personal faithfulness?

3. Despite Moses's doubts and insecurities, God continues to guide him (Exod 4:19–20). What fears or insecurities do you face when God calls you to step into a new role or responsibility? How can you grow in confidence and trust in God's plan (cf. Phil 4:13)?

4. Zipporah's actions highlight the importance of family in maintaining covenant faithfulness (Exod 4:25). How can families today work together to live out God's commands? What role does the family unit play in modeling covenant faithfulness within the community?

Exodus 5

Context and Analysis

Exodus 5 takes place after Moses and Aaron's first encounter with Pharaoh, in which they demand that Pharaoh let the Israelites go to worship God in the wilderness (Exod 5:1). Pharaoh's refusal and increased oppression of the Israelites serve as a turning point. Pharaoh not only denies their request but also increases the burden on the Israelites by forcing them to gather their own straw while still meeting the same brick quota (Exod 5:6–9). The Israelites' suffering intensifies, and Moses faces backlash from his people. Moses and Aaron boldly confront Pharaoh (Exod 5:1), but Pharaoh's response is one of defiance and cruelty (Exod 5:2–9). The Israelite overseers, caught between Moses's leadership and Pharaoh's harshness, feel betrayed when their workload increases (Exod 5:15–21). Moses, in turn, expresses frustration to God, questioning why the situation has worsened (Exod 5:22–23). Pharaoh repeatedly refers to the Israelites as "lazy" (Exod 5:8, 17), suggesting that their request to worship God is a pretext for escaping labor. This reveals a theme of control and power, as Pharaoh refuses to acknowledge God's authority. The use of the word "burden" highlights the Israelites' growing suffering.

Spiritual Insights: Basic Anxiety

The Israelites experience heightened anxiety and helplessness as their situation worsens (Exod 5:15–19). Their suffering is compounded by the failure of Moses and Aaron's initial attempts to secure their release. The Israelite overseers exhibit self-resignation, as they confront Pharaoh directly to plead for relief but are only met with further rejection (Exod 5:15–18). Moses, on the other hand, directs his anxiety toward God, questioning God's plan and expressing frustration (Exod 5:22–23). Moses begins to question whether God's plan will succeed after facing Pharaoh's resistance (Exod 5:22). This reveals a struggle between trusting God's timing and relying on immediate results. The Israelites, similarly, show signs of despair, losing faith in the possibility of liberation.

Problems and Dilemmas

Moses faces a spiritual dilemma as he wrestles with the apparent failure of God's plan. He struggles with the question of why God would allow things to worsen for the Israelites after promising deliverance (Exod 5:22–23). Moses's real self is revealed in his frustration and doubt. While he initially presented himself as God's appointed leader, the harsh realities of Pharaoh's resistance and the suffering of the Israelites expose his vulnerability. This section raises deeper questions about obedience and faith. How should Moses and the Israelites remain faithful to God's commands when their circumstances grow worse? The conflict between Pharaoh's oppression and God's promise of liberation intensifies, and it forces Moses to reevaluate his role as leader.

Themes and Obligations

The Israelites' vulnerability is heightened as Pharaoh increases their burdens (Exod 5:6–9). However, even in the midst of this suffering, God's promise of deliverance still stands, though it is not yet visible. Moses and Aaron are responsible for leading the Israelites, but their immediate failure to secure freedom raises questions about perseverance in leadership. They must remain committed to God's mission despite setbacks (Exod 5:22–23). The goal of liberating the Israelites is noble, but the harsh realities of Pharaoh's resistance reveal how challenging this pursuit will be. Moses's frustration shows that noble pursuits require endurance, especially when faced with opposition and failure.

Reflections and Application

Many today can relate to Moses's frustration when immediate results are not seen, especially when they believe they are following God's will (Exod 5:22–23). The passage speaks to those struggling with setbacks and discouragement, reminding them to trust in God's long-term plan. Moses expected immediate success when he confronted Pharaoh, but the reality of resistance challenges his expectations. This teaches us not to set unrealistic expectations for quick results, but rather to live faithfully, trusting in God's timing. In leadership and community challenges, setbacks often occur. Whether facing injustice, workplace difficulties, or family struggles, this passage encourages believers to persist in their calling, even when results are delayed or circumstances worsen.

God's Sovereignty and Providence

Despite Pharaoh's defiance and the worsening conditions, God's sovereignty is not diminished. Pharaoh's resistance sets the stage for the greater display of God's power in the coming plagues. Moses's frustration (Exod 5:22) is met later by God's assurance of victory (cf. Exod 6). Pharaoh's refusal to acknowledge God's authority (Exod 5:2) contrasts with Moses's growing understanding of God's power. The passage challenges readers to trust in God's authority, even when human leaders resist or oppose God's plans.

Covenant Relationship and Faithfulness

The Israelites' suffering, though intensified, only increases their reliance on God. Moses's dialogue with God reveals the importance of remembering that God's promises endure, even in moments of deep frustration and doubt (Exod 5:22–23). Moses's moment of doubt serves as a reminder to remain faithful to God's calling, even when immediate results are not visible. God's faithfulness to his covenant will ultimately prevail, though it requires patience and perseverance.

Human Vocation and Cultural Mandate

Moses is called to lead the Israelites, but the increased oppression from Pharaoh reveals how difficult this vocation will be (Exod 5:22–23). His calling involves confronting powerful opposition while maintaining trust in God's plan. This section shows that serving God's purposes often involves enduring hardship and setbacks. Leaders and communities must continue to cultivate faith and hope, even when the road to freedom or justice becomes more difficult.

Common Grace and Resistance to Evil

Pharaoh's harsh response represents the forces of evil and oppression, while Moses and Aaron represent God's redemptive plan. The tension between good and evil intensifies, and the need for divine intervention becomes more apparent (Exod 5:6-9). Moses and the Israelites face growing oppression, yet they are called to resist despair. God's grace operates even in the midst of suffering, calling his people to trust in his ultimate plan for justice and liberation (cf. Eph 6:10-13).

God's Grace and Redemptive History

This section highlights the beginning of God's plan to redeem Israel from slavery, even though Pharaoh's resistance initially causes increased suffering. God's grace is evident in his continued presence and plan, which will be revealed more fully in the plagues and eventual exodus. The passage challenges us to trust in God's redemptive work, even when our circumstances seem to worsen. God's grace will ultimately prevail, but the process may involve enduring suffering and opposition.

Cultural Mandate and Kingdom Work

The oppression of the Israelites under Pharaoh's harsh demands to produce more bricks without sufficient materials (Exod 5:7-9) reflects the exploitation of human labor and the perversion of work. In contrast, God's cultural mandate calls for work to be meaningful and a reflection of his creative order (cf. Gen 1:28). Pharaoh's treatment of the Israelites serves as a distortion of this mandate, and God's plan for their liberation is a restoration of their dignity and purpose in work. Moses and Aaron's mission to lead the Israelites to freedom is a form of kingdom work. They are called to be agents of renewal, delivering the people from unjust labor and into a life where they can worship God and fulfill their covenant responsibilities. Believers today are similarly called to be agents of renewal, working to restore justice and dignity in their communities and workplaces (cf. Matt 6:10).

Social Mandate and Family Life

Exodus 5 reflects the disruption of family and social life caused by Pharaoh's oppression. The increased burdens placed on the Israelites would have affected not only their work but also their ability to maintain healthy family relationships and community life. The chapter highlights the importance of justice and liberation in restoring the social order that God intends for his people. In contrast to Pharaoh's oppressive rule, God's deliverance of Israel is aimed at creating a community where families can flourish, and God's people can live in freedom and worship. This section reminds us of the importance of fighting for social and economic justice to support the flourishing of families and communities today (cf. Acts 2:42-47).

Liberty, Justice, and God's Kingdom

Exodus 5 reveals God's deep concern for justice as he begins to work through Moses to liberate his people from the political and economic oppression of Pharaoh. Pharaoh's unjust treatment of the Israelites demonstrates the kind of injustice that God opposes, and the chapter sets the stage for God's intervention on behalf of the oppressed. This calls believers to pursue justice in their own communities, standing against political, social, and economic injustice wherever it is found (cf. Mic 6:8). This section encourages us to engage in the pursuit of liberty and justice in a way that reflects God's kingdom. Just as Moses and Aaron confronted Pharaoh, we are called to confront injustice in our world. However, we must do so grounded in God's righteousness and guided by his wisdom, understanding that true justice comes from aligning with his will. Our pursuit of justice should reflect the values of the coming kingdom of God, where justice, mercy, and peace reign (cf. Matt 25:31-40).

Spiritual Warfare

Exodus 5 highlights the spiritual and moral challenges faced by Moses, Aaron, and the Israelites as they confront the oppressive power of Pharaoh. Moses's initial failure and the Israelites' increased suffering could easily lead to discouragement and doubt. However, the chapter also reveals the importance of perseverance in the face of spiritual and moral challenges. The opposition from Pharaoh can be seen as a form of spiritual warfare, where evil seeks to undermine God's plan for his people (cf. Eph 6:12). Believers today are called to stand firm in the face of similar moral and spiritual challenges, trusting in God's sovereignty even when opposition seems overwhelming. Just as Moses persevered through failure and doubt, we are encouraged to rely on God's strength and promises to overcome the challenges we face in pursuing his kingdom purposes (cf. 1 Cor 15:58).

Questions for Reflection and Discussion

1. Moses faces significant setbacks when Pharaoh increases the burdens on the Israelites (Exod 5:6–9). How do you handle setbacks or failures when pursuing God's calling in your life? What role does perseverance play in leadership, and how can you strengthen your trust in God during difficult times (cf. Jas 1:2–4)?

2. The Israelites experience greater oppression when Pharaoh refuses to listen to Moses and Aaron (Exod 5:7–9). How can we trust God when circumstances seem to worsen despite our efforts to seek justice or relief? What does this passage teach us about maintaining hope and faith in the face of injustice?

3. Moses expresses frustration and doubt to God, questioning why things have gotten worse (Exod 5:22–23). How do you respond when you feel like your efforts to follow God's will are not producing the desired results? How can this passage encourage you to bring your doubts and frustrations to God in prayer?

4. The Israelite overseers blame Moses and Aaron for worsening their situation (Exod 5:20–21). How can communities of faith support each other in times of suffering and oppression rather than turning against one another? What practical steps can we take to promote unity and perseverance during difficult times?

Exodus 6:1–27

Context and Analysis

This passage occurs after Moses's initial confrontation with Pharaoh, which resulted in the worsening of the Israelites' conditions. Pharaoh increased their labor, causing doubt and despair among the Israelites. In response, God reiterates his covenant promises, assuring Moses that he will deliver Israel by his mighty hand (Exod 6:1). The historical backdrop highlights the immense power imbalance between the Israelites, oppressed as slaves, and Pharaoh, who wields political power. The conflict centers on God's plan for Israel's redemption from slavery, which contrasts Pharaoh's human authority and oppression. Exodus 6:1–27 takes place after Moses's initial encounter with Pharaoh, which resulted in an increase in the oppression of the Israelites (Exod 5:6–18). The Israelites' condition worsens, and Moses questions God's plan. God responds by reaffirming his covenant promises and declares his intention to liberate the Israelites with his mighty hand (Exod 6:1–8). The genealogy of Moses and Aaron (Exod 6:14–27) links them to the Levitical lineage, demonstrating God's sovereign election of them for this role in the redemption of Israel. Moses struggles with fear and doubt, questioning why God allowed the situation to worsen (Exod 6:12). The Israelites, oppressed and in deep despair, are initially unable to accept Moses's reassurances (Exod 6:9). However, God's divine sovereignty and patience are emphasized as he reaffirms his promises to bring the people to freedom. The language of God's "mighty hand" (Exod 6:1) highlights divine intervention and control. God's self-revelation as Yahweh (Exod 6:2) underlines his authority over creation and history, as well as his covenantal faithfulness, which contrasts with the insecurity and fear felt by the Israelites and Moses.

Spiritual Insights: Basic Anxiety

Moses experiences significant doubt, feeling inadequate and questioning his role in God's plan (Exod 6:12). The Israelites, crushed under Pharaoh's oppression, are in a state of hopelessness, unable to trust in the promise of deliverance. Moses initially exhibits self-resignation, struggling with feelings of inadequacy and being overwhelmed by the apparent failure of his mission (Exod 6:12). However, God does not allow Moses to succumb to despair but encourages him by reminding him of the covenant and the divine promise. Both Moses and the Israelites are encouraged to shift their trust from their circumstances and abilities to God's sovereign power and faithfulness. Their anxiety and fear are rooted in their human limitations, but God directs them to focus on his redemptive work.

Problems and Dilemmas

Moses faces the dilemma of continuing his obedience in the face of overwhelming opposition and personal doubt. Should he continue to trust in God's promises despite his insecurities, or should he give up on his mission? The Israelites, on the other hand, are faced with the challenge of trusting God's promises in the midst of intensified suffering. Moses is called to lead, yet he grapples with his perceived inadequacies (Exod 6:12). This passage highlights the tension between Moses's true self (a flawed, doubting leader) and the idealized vision of himself as God's chosen leader. God's patience with Moses underscores that God's calling is not dependent on human perfection but on divine grace. The deeper conflict is between human fear and divine assurance. Moses and the Israelites are both challenged to rely on God's promises in the face of worsening circumstances, testing their obedience and faith.

Themes and Obligations

This passage emphasizes the contrast between human vulnerability and divine protection. Despite Pharaoh's power and the intensifying oppression, God's promise to deliver his people is unwavering (Exod 6:6). Moses and the Israelites are called to trust in God's protection rather than rely on their own strength. This text places on its audience the responsibility to trust God's covenant promises even when circumstances seem dire. It challenges readers to act with faithfulness and perseverance, trusting in God's ultimate authority over earthly powers. Moses is hindered by fear, which keeps him from fully embracing his role. His calling is noble, yet it is fear and doubt that threaten to undermine his ability to fulfill God's plan.

Reflections and Application

Like Moses, many today face struggles with inadequacy or fear of failure, particularly in the face of seemingly insurmountable challenges. This passage speaks to the importance of trusting in God's faithfulness and power, even when circumstances suggest otherwise. God's promise remains sure, and he is sovereign over all challenges. In our modern world, there is often an unrealistic drive for perfection, especially in spiritual leadership or faith. Moses's doubts remind us that God works through flawed individuals and that trust in him, not human perfection, is what brings about his purposes.

Application Today: This passage can apply to leadership roles, where leaders might feel overwhelmed or inadequate. It speaks to the importance of trusting God's guidance in moments of failure, understanding that ultimate success comes from his hand, not from human strength or ability.

God's Sovereignty and Providence

Exodus 6:1–12 makes clear God's absolute sovereignty and providence over all creation. God's reiteration of his covenant promises in this chapter reaffirms his control over history and his ability to bring about his plans, despite human obstacles (Exod 6:6–8). Pharaoh's resistance and the increased burden on the Israelites do not undermine God's ultimate plan.

Application Today: Believers today can take comfort in the sovereignty of God, knowing that even in the face of apparent setbacks, God's purposes will prevail. This section encourages submission to God's will in personal and societal leadership, recognizing that God's hand is guiding history toward his redemptive ends (cf. Rom 8:28).

Covenant Relationship and Faithfulness

God reminds Moses of his covenant with Abraham, Isaac, and Jacob, emphasizing his faithfulness to that covenant despite current circumstances (Exod 6:2–5). The covenantal relationship between God and his people is the foundation for their deliverance. This section calls believers to live in faithfulness to God's covenant promises. Just as God remembered his covenant with Israel, he remains faithful to his covenant with his people today.

This encourages believers to persevere in faith, trusting that God will fulfill his promises in their own lives and communities (cf. Heb 10:23).

Human Vocation and Cultural Mandate

In this passage, God reminds Moses of his divine calling to lead the Israelites out of Egypt (Exod 6:6-7). Moses's vocation as a leader is not merely a political or social responsibility but a deeply spiritual one that ties into the broader cultural mandate. God is calling Moses to cultivate justice and restoration by liberating Israel from Pharaoh's oppressive reign. This liberation will eventually allow Israel to fulfill its covenantal role as a kingdom of priests and a holy nation (cf. Exod 19:6), demonstrating the cultural mandate's role in human flourishing.

Application Today: This section calls believers to align their vocations and work with God's mission to cultivate justice, righteousness, and peace in the world. Whether through secular work, ministry, or family life, every believer is called to participate in God's kingdom-building work. Stewardship of creation includes not only physical resources but also social, political, and spiritual responsibilities. In today's context, Christians are called to work toward justice, equality, and mercy in their various spheres of influence, reflecting God's kingdom purposes in the world (cf. Col 3:23-24).

Common Grace and Resistance to Evil

This section shows the tension between Pharaoh's evil oppression and God's redemptive plan. Even though Pharaoh continues to resist God's commands, God's grace is working to bring about deliverance for his people. God's response to Moses in verses 6-8 is a declaration of his redemptive purpose: to bring Israel out of Egypt and into a land of their own, thereby reversing the effects of their suffering. God's redemptive plan demonstrates his common grace working within a broken world to resist and eventually overcome the evil represented by Pharaoh's regime.

Application Today: Christians today are called to resist evil in its various forms—whether in personal sin, societal injustice, or political oppression—while recognizing that all good things come from God's grace. Believers participate in God's mission by actively opposing evil, whether through advocacy, ministry, or personal righteousness. This resistance is not only political but also spiritual, as believers are engaged in a cosmic battle against evil forces (cf. Eph 6:12). However, Christians must rely on

God's grace as the source of strength and not fall into despair when faced with persistent evil, trusting that God's ultimate justice will prevail.

God's Grace and Redemptive History

In this chapter, God's grace is explicitly shown as he reaffirms his covenant promises and declares his intent to redeem Israel (Exod 6:6). God's gracious intervention in history is a key theme as he moves toward the fulfillment of his redemptive plan, beginning with the exodus. God's grace not only initiates Israel's liberation but also sustains them through the challenges ahead. His deliverance is rooted in the covenant he made with Abraham, Isaac, and Jacob, and it extends forward to the ultimate redemptive act in Christ (cf. Gal 3:29). This section encourages believers to trust in God's grace, knowing that it is the foundation of their salvation and ongoing sanctification. God's redemptive work in Exodus points to his ultimate redemptive plan through Jesus Christ. Believers today are part of this ongoing narrative of grace, called to live in light of God's work of redemption. This informs how Christians engage in societal and cultural issues, knowing that God's grace is at work even in difficult circumstances and that the ultimate victory belongs to him (cf. Titus 2:11-14).

Cultural Mandate and Kingdom Work

The cultural mandate—to cultivate, steward, and develop creation—is implicit in God's promise to bring Israel out of Egypt and lead them to the promised land (Exod 6:6-8). God's intention for Israel is not only their physical liberation but also their restoration to a place where they can flourish, worship, and steward the land. The purpose of their redemption is so they can fulfill their calling as his covenant people, to reflect his glory through their lives and communities.

Application Today: This passage informs our calling to participate in God's mission of restoration. We are called to cultivate and steward, not just the physical environment but also relationships, communities, and societal structures, aligning them with God's kingdom purposes. In work and rest, Christians are agents of renewal, working to restore what has been broken by sin and oppression. In our engagement with the world, we are to mirror the deliverance of Israel by seeking justice, promoting human dignity, and caring for creation, knowing that God's sovereignty extends over all aspects of life (cf. Col 3:23).

Social Mandate and Family Life

This section highlights the importance of the family in God's covenantal framework. God's promise to Israel is rooted in his covenant with the patriarchs—Abraham, Isaac, and Jacob—signifying that his work of redemption extends across generations (Exod 6:5). The family is foundational to God's covenant people, as seen in his concern for their well-being and flourishing within a just society.

Application Today: The role of families in shaping communities and upholding God's order is central. Strong families are the building blocks of a strong society. Godly families teach children the fear of the LORD (cf. Deut 6:6-7) and raise the next generation to carry on the work of justice, mercy, and stewardship. In today's world, upholding biblical values in family life is critical for advancing God's purposes. This involves nurturing faith, teaching responsibility, and fostering community-oriented values that reflect the covenantal relationship between God and his people.

Liberty, Justice, and God's Kingdom

God's declaration in this passage reveals his deep concern for justice, particularly political and economic liberty. The oppression of the Israelites under Pharaoh represents an unjust political and economic system. God promises to bring judgment upon Egypt and to liberate Israel (Exod 6:6), demonstrating that true justice comes from God's righteousness. His goal is not just the physical freedom of his people but also the establishment of a just society where they can live as his free, covenant people. This section calls believers to pursue justice grounded in God's righteousness. Just as God opposed Pharaoh's exploitation of the Israelites, Christians today must engage in the fight for justice, standing against oppression, economic disenfranchisement, and political tyranny. We are called to reflect God's heart for liberty and righteousness, not through human power alone but through actions that are guided by his word and empowered by his Spirit. In doing so, we point toward the coming kingdom of God, where justice and righteousness will reign (cf. Isa 61:1-2; Luke 4:18-19).

Spiritual Warfare

Moses, faced with the growing opposition of Pharaoh and the increasing suffering of the Israelites, struggles with doubt and despair (Exod 6:9-12). The spiritual battle here is not only against the physical oppression of Pharaoh but also against the doubt and discouragement that can arise when God's promises seem delayed. God reassures Moses and reaffirms his covenant, encouraging Moses to remain steadfast in his mission despite the obstacles.

Application Today: This passage teaches us about the spiritual warfare involved in standing firm in God's promises, even when circumstances are discouraging. Believers must maintain moral integrity and faith, knowing that spiritual warfare often involves resisting the temptation to doubt God's timing or purposes. In moments of struggle, we are to hold fast to God's word and the knowledge that he is sovereign, even when facing powerful earthly forces. This section equips us to stand firm in the face of both external opposition and internal fear, trusting that God is working out his redemptive plan (cf. Eph 6:10–18).

God's Concern for Justice and Liberty

In Exod 6:1–27, God's concern for justice and liberty is explicitly revealed in his promise to deliver the Israelites from their political and economic bondage under Pharaoh. God states, "I will bring you out from under the yoke of the Egyptians. I will free you from being slaves to them" (Exod 6:6). This divine declaration highlights God's opposition to tyranny and unjust rule. God does not tolerate the oppression of his people under a coercive regime, and he moves to restore their liberty through his power.

This passage shows that freedom from oppressive rule is central to God's justice. Pharaoh represents an authoritarian regime that suppresses the liberties of the Israelites, exploiting their labor for his economic gain. God's intervention underscores the principle that rulers who violate the freedom and dignity of individuals act contrary to God's righteous order. Just as God rescues Israel from the unjust dominion of Egypt, Christians are called to advocate for systems of governance that respect individual liberty, limited government, and the inherent dignity of each person.

In the New Testament, Paul echoes this idea of freedom in Gal 5:1, where he writes, "It is for freedom that Christ has set us free. Stand firm, then, and do not let yourselves be burdened again by a yoke of slavery." While this refers primarily to spiritual freedom, it also applies to the broader concept of liberty from any form of oppression, including unjust political and economic systems.

Pursuing Justice Today, Grounded in God's Righteousness

This section calls believers to pursue justice that is grounded in God's righteousness, not human definitions of justice alone. God's justice in Exod 6 is not just about freeing the Israelites from political slavery; it is about fulfilling his covenantal promise to restore them as his people (Exod 6:7–8). God's justice always aims at both liberation and righteousness, combining political freedom with moral responsibility under God's law. For some, pursuing justice today means advocating for minimal government interference in people's lives while ensuring that every individual's dignity and rights are respected. Systems that allow for individual freedom, economic liberty, and personal responsibility align with the biblical vision of justice, which allows people to flourish under God's design without oppressive control.

In terms of practical application, Mic 6:8 provides a framework for this pursuit: "He has shown you, O mortal, what is good. And what does the Lord require of you? To act justly and to love mercy and to walk humbly with your God." Justice grounded in God's righteousness calls for action against oppressive systems, but it must also be tempered with mercy and humility.

Engaging in the Pursuit of Liberty in a Way That Reflects God's Kingdom

In Exod 6, God's promise to liberate the Israelites reflects his broader plan for establishing a kingdom of justice, righteousness, and peace. As God prepares to deliver Israel, he declares that they will no longer be slaves but his people, bound in a covenant relationship with him (Exod 6:7). This points to a deeper reality: true liberty is not just freedom from political oppression but freedom to live in obedience to God's righteous rule. For Christians today, this means that while we engage in the pursuit of liberty in political, social, or economic arenas, it must always be framed within the vision of God's coming kingdom. Liberty for liberty's sake is not the ultimate goal; rather, liberty should lead to the flourishing of individuals in a society where God's justice, peace, and truth reign. Jesus speaks to this kingdom-centered vision of freedom in Matt 6:33: "But seek first his kingdom and his righteousness, and all these things will be given to you as well." Believers are to seek liberty in a way that reflects the values of God's kingdom—liberty that is tied to righteousness, justice, and the common good, not just individual self-interest.

Questions for Reflection and Discussion

1. How does God's promise to free Israel from Egyptian oppression in Exod 6 shape our understanding of justice today? What lessons can we draw for engaging with unjust political, economic, or social systems around us?

2. In what ways does the liberation described in Exod 6 reflect a deeper spiritual freedom that God desires for his people? How can we balance pursuing personal liberty with promoting the common good?

3. How does God's reassurance to Moses in Exod 6 help you trust in his promises amid life's challenges? How can we practically demonstrate trust in God's redemptive purposes when facing difficulties?

4. Exodus 6 highlights God's active role in rescuing and restoring his people. What does it look like for us today to actively participate in God's mission of restoration and justice in society? Provide specific examples relevant to your own context.

5. Considering God's covenant promises in Exod 6, how does our role as stewards of God's creation influence the way we approach our daily work or vocation? What actions can we take to reflect God's kingdom values in our responsibilities?

6. Exodus 6 presents God's opposition to Pharaoh's oppressive rule. How can we, individually or as communities, actively resist evil and injustice while relying on God's grace rather than our own strength? Share practical steps applicable in your life.

Exodus 6:28—7:13

Context and Analysis

In Exod 6:28—7:13, God commands Moses and Aaron to confront Pharaoh again and demand the release of the Israelites. The historical background centers on Israel's enslavement in Egypt, where Pharaoh's refusal to obey God leads to escalating conflicts between divine power and human resistance. The cultural context highlights the Egyptian belief in Pharaoh as a divine ruler and their polytheistic worldview, which clashes with the Israelites' monotheistic faith in Yahweh. Moses, still insecure about his speaking abilities (Exod 6:30), obeys God's command. Pharaoh, meanwhile, embodies resistance to God's authority, and his magicians mimic Aaron's miracles, creating an illusion of control. Yet, Aaron's staff, turned into a serpent and swallowing the magicians' staffs (Exod 7:12), symbolizes God's ultimate authority over human power. The repetition of themes such as hardening of hearts (Exod 7:3) and signs and wonders highlights the divine control over the situation.

Spiritual Insights: Basic Anxiety

Moses continues to experience anxiety about his role, expressing concerns about his lack of eloquence (Exod 6:30). His fear of failure and inadequacy stems from his earlier rejection by both the Israelites and Pharaoh. Pharaoh's anxiety revolves around losing control over the Israelites, leading to his hardened heart and further rebellion against God (Exod 7:3). Moses ultimately trusts God, despite his insecurity, learning to rely on God's provision. Pharaoh demonstrates self-expansion by relying on his magicians and his own perceived authority, rejecting God's sovereignty. Their responses illustrate the battle between trusting in human power versus divine providence.

Problems and Dilemmas

Several spiritual and moral dilemmas emerge in this passage: Moses wrestles with his fear but submits to God, while Pharaoh chooses to harden his heart despite witnessing God's power. Pharaoh's magicians imitate God's miracles, revealing the human tendency to trust in false powers rather than the true God. The tension between obedience and resistance reveals deeper questions about leadership, freedom, and divine authority.

Themes and Obligations

Moses and Aaron are vulnerable messengers confronting the powerful Pharaoh, yet God's provision and protection are evident through the signs and wonders he performs (Exod 7:10–12). This highlights the lesson that even when facing powerful opposition, trusting in God's provision is essential. Pharaoh's responsibility to recognize God's authority contrasts with his hardened heart. Moses's faithfulness to God's command shows that our duty is to obey God's calling, despite our fears or the power structures that oppose us.

Reflections and Application

This passage speaks to modern struggles with insecurity and leadership. Moses's fear of failure resonates with anyone who feels inadequate for a task, but his reliance on God reminds us to depend on divine strength. Pharaoh's resistance to God's authority warns against the dangers of pride and self-reliance.

Application Today: This passage applies to contexts of leadership and social justice: Are we following God's calling to confront injustice and trust in his power, or are we relying on human systems and false powers?

God's Sovereignty and Providence

God's sovereignty is displayed in his control over the events leading up to Israel's deliverance. Despite Pharaoh's resistance, God is fully in charge, orchestrating events according to his will. This passage encourages believers to trust that God is sovereign over all leaders and systems of power (Exod

7:3). The New Testament reflects this sovereignty in Jesus's authority over all things (Matt 28:18).

Covenant Relationship and Faithfulness

God's covenant faithfulness to Israel is evident in this passage, where he renews his commitment to deliver his people from bondage (Exod 6:6–8). Moses and Aaron's role as mediators reflects the covenant responsibility to act on God's behalf. This passage calls believers to trust in God's covenant promises and to live faithfully in response.

Human Vocation and Cultural Mandate

Moses and Aaron fulfill their vocation as leaders and mediators between God and his people. This passage reflects the cultural mandate by showing that God's people are called to exercise leadership and stewardship in a fallen world, confronting evil powers and speaking truth to those in authority. For modern believers, this is a call to engage in society, upholding justice and truth as part of God's kingdom work (Eph 6:10–18).

Common Grace and Resistance to Evil

The signs and wonders that God performs through Moses and Aaron serve as a demonstration of God's grace in the midst of evil. Pharaoh's magicians represent false power, but God's truth prevails. This passage calls believers to recognize and resist the false powers in society, knowing that God's grace sustains his people in the face of evil.

God's Grace and Redemptive History

This section is part of God's larger redemptive plan, moving toward the deliverance of Israel from Egypt. God's grace is evident in his patience with Moses, his empowerment of Aaron, and his demonstration of power over Pharaoh. In the New Testament, this points to Jesus, who ultimately delivers humanity from sin and death (Col 2:15). Believers today are called to participate in God's redemptive work, addressing social and cultural issues with the hope of God's ultimate victory.

Questions for Reflection and Discussion

1. How does Moses's fear and insecurity resonate with our own struggles in leadership or faith? What steps can we take to trust God more fully when faced with daunting tasks?

2. In what ways do we see modern-day Pharaohs—people or systems—resisting God's authority? How can we as Christians confront these powers while relying on God's strength?

3. What does this passage teach us about the difference between true and false power? How can we discern God's truth in a world filled with deception and false promises?

4. How does God's covenant faithfulness to Israel encourage us to be faithful in our responsibilities, both personally and within our communities? How can we better engage in God's kingdom work in today's society?

Exodus 7:13—11:10

Context and Analysis

This section of Exodus recounts the plagues God brought upon Egypt in response to Pharaoh's hardened heart and refusal to let the Israelites go (Exod 7:13). The Egyptian empire, which had enslaved the Israelites, was a dominant political and cultural force at the time, and Pharaoh was seen as both a political and divine figure. The plagues, then, are a direct confrontation of God's sovereignty over Pharaoh's supposed divine authority and the Egyptian gods. Pharaoh's heart is hardened (Exod 7:13, 8:19, 9:12), leading to his refusal to obey God's command. Moses and Aaron, though initially reluctant, faithfully follow God's instructions to bring his message of liberation to Pharaoh (Exod 7:10). The Egyptian magicians attempt to mimic God's signs but eventually confess that the plagues are from "the finger of God" (Exod 8:19). The phrase "Let my people go" (Exod 7:16; 8:1, 20) emphasizes God's demand for justice and freedom for his people. Pharaoh's hardening of heart is repeated as a symbol of human resistance to divine authority and control, contrasting God's sovereignty with human rebellion.

Spiritual Insights: Basic Anxiety

Pharaoh's anxiety stems from fear of losing control and power. His hardening heart shows his refusal to submit to God's authority, reflecting the human tendency to cling to power rather than trust God. The plagues themselves create fear and insecurity in the hearts of the Egyptians as their land, livestock, and bodies are affected by the plagues (Exod 9:3–6, 9). Pharaoh's self-expansion seeks to maintain dominance over Israel despite the devastation of the plagues (Exod 9:7). Pharaoh briefly concedes and asks for Moses to pray to God to end certain plagues, but he does not submit fully (Exod 9:27–28). Pharaoh's reliance on his magicians and his own stubbornness demonstrates his refusal to trust in God's authority.

Problems and Dilemmas

Pharaoh's refusal to free the Israelites despite witnessing God's power raises the moral question of human pride versus submission to divine authority. The text illustrates the dangers of resisting God's call for justice and liberation, not only for Pharaoh but for the Egyptian people. Pharaoh's idealized self-image as a god-king is shattered by God's plagues. His inability to let go of this false identity leads to his eventual downfall, showing the danger of clinging to an idealized self instead of embracing the reality of God's sovereignty. The conflict between Pharaoh's authority and God's divine command exposes deeper questions of obedience and leadership. Why does Pharaoh resist the call to free the Israelites despite clear evidence of God's power? His hardened heart reveals a spiritual battle of pride and rebellion.

Themes and Obligations

The Israelites are portrayed as vulnerable slaves, but God's protection of them through the plagues, while sparing them from certain plagues (Exod 8:22; 9:4, 26), highlights his divine care for his covenant people. In contrast, Egypt's vulnerability to God's wrath demonstrates human helplessness in the face of divine power. The passage places a moral burden on Pharaoh to act justly and release the Israelites. His refusal exemplifies how human leaders are accountable to God for their actions. For the Israelites, this text reinforces their duty to trust in God's deliverance, even in the face of prolonged suffering.

Reflections and Application

Pharaoh's fear of losing power mirrors contemporary anxieties about control and authority in personal and societal contexts. The lesson here is that clinging to power in defiance of God's will leads to destruction, whereas submission to God brings liberation. Pharaoh's refusal to acknowledge God and his persistent belief in his own invincibility can be seen in today's societal struggles with pride and self-reliance. This passage challenges us to abandon unattainable self-images and rely on God's sovereignty.

Application Today: Leaders today face similar temptations to resist pursuing justice for the sake of maintaining control. This passage calls modern leaders to submit to God's will and work for the flourishing of all people under their authority. For individuals, it calls for trust in God's timing and deliverance in situations of oppression.

God's Sovereignty and Providence

The plagues clearly demonstrate God's sovereign control over nature, human affairs, and political powers (Exod 9:14–16). Pharaoh's power is shown to be limited in comparison to the creator of the universe. God's intervention in Egypt is a powerful reminder that he controls history and human destiny. Recognizing God's sovereignty in both personal and societal leadership encourages believers to submit to his will in every area of life. It reminds us that no earthly authority can thwart God's ultimate purposes.

Covenant Relationship and Faithfulness

God's actions throughout the plagues reaffirm his commitment to the covenant he made with Abraham, Isaac, and Jacob to deliver their descendants from bondage (Exod 6:5). His faithfulness to Israel underscores that he keeps his promises, even through trials and suffering. This faithfulness challenges believers to remain faithful in their covenant relationship with God. Trust in his promises should shape how we live and interact with our communities, knowing that God is always working for the good of his people.

Human Vocation and Cultural Mandate

Moses and Aaron are called to carry out God's mandate to lead the Israelites to freedom. Their obedience to God's call shows how human vocation aligns with the divine mission of liberation and stewardship of creation (Exod 7:6).

Application Today: Believers are called to participate in God's mission by serving their communities, working for justice, and caring for creation. Our vocations should reflect God's purposes, aligning with his desire for the renewal of all things.

Questions for Reflection and Discussion

1. How does Pharaoh's resistance to God's commands reflect human tendencies to cling to power and control? How can we guard against such tendencies in our own lives?

2. What lessons can we learn about leadership and justice from Moses and Aaron's obedience versus Pharaoh's disobedience? How can we apply these lessons in our communities and workplaces?

3. How does the story of the plagues challenge our understanding of suffering and deliverance? How can we trust in God's sovereignty in the face of personal and societal struggles today?

4. In what ways does this passage call us to examine our own pride and areas where we resist God's will? How can we cultivate a heart of submission to God's authority in both our personal lives and societal roles?

Cultural Mandate and Kingdom Work

In this passage, the cultural mandate to steward and cultivate creation is highlighted in the way Moses and Aaron engage with Pharaoh, representing God's will for the proper ordering of society. The plagues, in particular, show God's control over nature (water, land, animals) and his judgment on how Egypt misused its power and wealth at the expense of the Israelites (Exod 7:14–21; 8:1–7). The Nile turning to blood, the plagues of frogs, gnats, and flies, and the other natural calamities are direct interventions by God, revealing that creation itself responds to God's will.

Application Today: As Christians, we are called to responsibly steward creation, acknowledging that it belongs to God. The work we do—whether in business, family, or society—must reflect a desire to cultivate the world in a way that honors God's purposes, aligns with his justice, and works toward restoration (Rom 8:19–21).

Social Mandate and Family Life

This section also shows the breakdown of family and community life within Egypt as a result of Pharaoh's oppressive policies and refusal to let the Israelites go. The plagues affect not just individuals but entire households (Exod 9:6, 26), including the devastating loss of the firstborn in Egypt. Meanwhile,

God is preserving Israel's families and working to redeem them from oppression (Exod 10:23).

Application Today: The passage highlights the importance of maintaining the integrity of family life under God's design. The preservation of Israel's families contrasts with the destruction in Egypt, illustrating how God upholds family and community structures. We are called to promote godly families and communities, ensuring that the social fabric reflects God's order and justice. This involves defending vulnerable families and resisting societal structures that oppress or undermine God's order for families.

Liberty, Justice, and God's Kingdom

God's actions in this passage demonstrate his deep concern for justice and liberty, particularly as he seeks to liberate the Israelites from political and economic bondage (Exod 7:16, 9:1). The plagues reveal God's justice in action, confronting Pharaoh's oppression and refusal to recognize the divine right of the Israelites to be free. The plagues themselves are acts of divine judgment against an unjust regime, showing God's commitment to establishing justice on earth. This passage affirms the pursuit of liberty as a reflection of God's desire for human flourishing, grounded in his righteousness. God's intervention demonstrates that unjust systems of power and oppression are ultimately subject to his authority. Christians are called to engage in the pursuit of justice and liberty in society, advocating for political and economic systems that reflect God's righteousness and protect individual freedoms, particularly for the marginalized.

Spiritual Warfare

The battle between Pharaoh and God is not a political or social one; it is a spiritual conflict. Pharaoh's refusal to let the Israelites go is ultimately a rejection of God's authority and moral order. The plagues are signs of God's power over the false gods of Egypt, revealing the spiritual warfare behind the conflict (Exod 8:19, 9:14). Pharaoh's hardened heart (Exod 9:12) is a symbol of the moral and spiritual rebellion that exists in opposition to God's kingdom. For believers today, this passage teaches us that spiritual warfare is ongoing, and we must stand firm in our integrity, resisting the powers that seek to undermine God's moral and spiritual authority. The New Testament echoes this battle in Eph 6:12, where Paul writes that our struggle is not against flesh and blood, but against spiritual forces of evil. We are called to equip ourselves with God's armor, living with moral integrity in a world that is in constant opposition to God's kingdom.

Questions for Reflection and Discussion

1. What do the escalating plagues reveal about the nature of God's justice and patience? How does this challenge or affirm your view of divine judgment in the face of human stubbornness?

2. How do the signs and wonders in these chapters serve to distinguish the God of Israel from the gods of Egypt? In what ways do we still struggle today with trusting in the living God over modern idols of power, success, or security?

3. How does God's repeated act of making a distinction between Egypt and Israel help us understand his covenantal faithfulness? What does this say about the identity and responsibility of God's people today?

4. What role does intergenerational testimony play in this passage (see Exod 10:1–2)? How can we ensure that our own children and communities remember and recount God's acts of justice, mercy, and power?

Exodus 12:1–30

Context and Analysis

This passage details the first Passover, which is the turning point in Israel's deliverance from Egyptian slavery. The historical context highlights the final plague, the death of the firstborn, and God's instructions to Moses and Aaron for Israel's salvation (Exod 12:12–13). The cultural practice of the Passover meal—a lamb without blemish, blood applied to doorposts, and unleavened bread—was established as a lasting ordinance (Exod 12:14). The Israelites respond in obedience to God's command, applying the blood to their homes (Exod 12:28), while Pharaoh's hardened heart leads to further destruction. Pharaoh responds to the loss of his firstborn with fear and vulnerability, finally relenting and allowing the Israelites to leave (Exod 12:31–32). Key symbols include the blood of the lamb, representing God's provision of salvation (Exod 12:7, 13), and the unleavened bread, symbolizing the haste of their deliverance. These symbols foreshadow themes of control, fear, and divine intervention, especially in relation to God's ultimate control over life and death.

Spiritual Insights: Basic Anxiety

The Israelites experience fear and anxiety as they prepare for the final plague. The command to mark their homes with blood reveals their vulnerability and trust in God's promise (Exod 12:7, 23). Pharaoh, too, experiences fear but hardens his heart throughout the plagues, only relenting after the death of the firstborn (Exod 12:30). Pharaoh exemplifies more self-expansive tendencies, trying to maintain control by resisting God's commands (Exod 12:29–31). The Israelites place their trust in God's instructions, acting in faith despite their fear (Exod 12:28).

Problems and Dilemmas

The moral dilemma in this passage revolves around obedience to God's instruction and the consequences of disobedience. The Israelites must trust God's command, even as they witness the death of the Egyptian firstborns. Pharaoh faces the dilemma of continuing in rebellion or yielding to God's authority (Exod 12:31-32). The Israelites are called to embrace their identity as God's chosen people and trust in his protection. Pharaoh's idealized self is one of power and control, yet his resistance only leads to destruction. Questions about God's justice and mercy arise—why the Egyptian firstborn must die while Israel is spared through the blood of the lamb. This highlights God's sovereign will in redemptive history.

Themes and Obligations

This passage illustrates the theme of divine protection, as the Israelites are shielded from death by the blood of the lamb (Exod 12:13, 23). It shows the stark contrast between God's provision for his people and the vulnerability of those outside his covenant. The Israelites' responsibility is to obey God's command to observe the Passover and apply the blood (Exod 12:21-22). This act of obedience signifies trust in God's provision and calls readers to reflect on their duty to follow God's commands, even when uncertain of the outcomes.

Reflections and Application

The fear of death and uncertainty seen in the Israelites parallels modern struggles with insecurity and fear. The lesson here is one of trusting God's provision, even when it seems irrational or when we face peril. Pharaoh's relentless attempt to control the situation despite clear signs of divine authority mirrors how we often cling to power or ideals that are unattainable, leading to failure. This passage teaches us to yield to God's will rather than pursuing unattainable ideals.

God's Sovereignty and Providence

This section showcases God's sovereign control over life, death, and the unfolding of history. The Passover demonstrates God's providence in sparing Israel while bringing judgment on Egypt (Exod 12:12-13). His sovereignty is revealed in every plague, and his ability to control even the heart of Pharaoh shows his ultimate authority (Rom 9:17–18).

Application Today: Trust in God's sovereignty should shape our submission to his will in every aspect of life, whether personal or societal. He remains in control of both deliverance and judgment, calling us to trust him fully.

Covenant Relationship and Faithfulness

This section deeply reflects the covenant relationship between God and Israel. The Passover becomes a sign of God's faithfulness to his covenant promises (Exod 12:24–25). The blood of the lamb prefigures the new covenant in Christ (Luke 22:20), where Jesus, as the true Passover Lamb, seals the new covenant with his blood (1 Cor 5:7).

Human Vocation and Cultural Mandate

The observance of the Passover can be seen as an act of cultural memory and identity. It reminds Israel of their special calling to live as a redeemed people (Exod 12:17). The cultural mandate here aligns with their mission to steward this redemption story and pass it down through generations (Exod 12:26–27).

Application Today: As believers today, we are called to live out our vocation as God's people, preserving and cultivating the message of redemption in both work and rest, in the family and in the broader world.

Common Grace and Resistance to Evil

This passage portrays the tension between good and evil as God brings judgment on the Egyptian oppressors and liberates his people (Exod 12:12). The plagues demonstrate God's grace in preserving his people while judging wickedness. Even in this, Pharaoh is given opportunities to repent, but he resists (Exod 12:29–30).

God's Grace and Redemptive History

The Passover is a monumental event in redemptive history, pointing forward to Christ, the ultimate Passover Lamb. Through the blood of the lamb, Israel is spared from death, foreshadowing how the blood of Christ spares believers from eternal death (John 1:29; 1 Pet 1:18–19). This section teaches us to trust in the redemptive work of God in Christ and to live out the implications of that redemption in our everyday lives.

Cultural Mandate and Kingdom Work

In Exod 12:1–30, the Passover event emphasizes how God's people are to live in response to his redemptive work. The cultural mandate of cultivating, stewarding, and developing creation is highlighted through Israel's call to remember the Passover as an annual observance (Exod 12:14, 17). This stewardship of memory and tradition ensures that each generation recognizes God's deliverance and his sovereignty over creation. The Israelites are also instructed to prepare their homes and families for the coming of the Lord's deliverance by carefully following the commands given regarding the Passover lamb and the unleavened bread (Exod 12:3–11). This teaches us about stewardship in work, as we are called to act with diligence, preparation, and obedience in our daily vocations. As we participate in God's mission of restoring all things, we are reminded that our work, even in mundane tasks, serves to reflect God's redemptive work and points toward the ultimate renewal of all creation.

Application Today: In the modern context, we are called to live out the kingdom mandate in our daily lives, cultivating good works and stewarding the resources and opportunities God has given us. This includes work and rest patterns that honor God and reflect his ongoing mission of restoration (Col 3:23–24).

Social Mandate and Family Life

Exodus 12:1–30 places a strong emphasis on family and community involvement in the Passover celebration. Each household was responsible for selecting a lamb, preparing it, and eating it together (Exod 12:3–4). The family structure is central to the communal life of Israel, and God's instructions to commemorate this event as a family-based celebration show the importance of the family unit in transmitting faith from one generation to the next (Exod 12:24–27). This passage teaches us that family life and social structures are foundational in advancing God's purposes. The family is a primary context for teaching and living out covenant faithfulness. Through the Passover, parents are instructed to tell their children the story of God's redemption, fostering a generational connection to God's acts in history (Exod 12:26–27).

Application Today: In today's world, we are called to uphold God's order in family and society by fostering godly homes, teaching our children about God's saving acts, and strengthening our communities through shared worship and remembrance. This reflects the Reformed emphasis on the family as a critical sphere for spiritual growth and cultural influence (Deut 6:6-9).

Liberty, Justice, and God's Kingdom

Exodus 12 highlights God's deep concern for justice and liberty. The Passover is the climactic event of God's deliverance of the Israelites from slavery, a political and economic liberation that reflects his justice. The death of the Egyptian firstborns (Exod 12:29) is a manifestation of God's righteous judgment against Pharaoh's oppression and resistance to his will. At the same time, the Israelites are spared by the blood of the lamb, demonstrating God's mercy and justice working together (Exod 12:13). This passage calls us to pursue justice today, grounded in God's righteousness. The deliverance from Egypt reminds us that God is always concerned with the liberation of the oppressed and that justice is a central aspect of his kingdom. As God's people, we are called to engage in actions that reflect his justice, including fighting for political and economic liberty where oppression exists, and doing so in a way that points to the coming kingdom of God, where perfect justice will reign.

Application Today: In contemporary contexts, this may mean working for justice in our communities, standing against oppression, and advocating for systems that reflect God's righteousness and care for all people (Mic 6:8).

Spiritual Warfare

The events of Exod 12 reveal a battle between God's kingdom and the kingdom of darkness. Pharaoh's resistance to God's commands reflects the spiritual opposition to God's purposes, and the plagues, culminating in the death of the firstborn, show the extent of this spiritual warfare (Exod 12:29-30). The Passover, however, demonstrates that victory comes through obedience and faith in God's provision—the blood of the lamb. This passage teaches that God's people must remain faithful and vigilant in the face of spiritual and moral challenges. The Israelites' act of faith in applying the blood and following God's instructions (Exod 12:28) serves as a model for how we are to confront spiritual warfare today. By trusting in God's provision and living in obedience, we engage in the battle against sin and the forces of evil.

Application Today: For believers today, this means standing firm in faith and resisting the spiritual powers that seek to lead us away from God's purposes (Eph 6:12–13). Moral integrity is essential, as we are called to live in a way that reflects God's holiness and redemptive power in a world often hostile to his kingdom.

Questions for Reflection and Discussion

1. How does the Passover reveal God's justice and mercy, and how should that shape the way we pursue justice and mercy in our communities today?

2. What does the importance of family and community in the Passover celebration teach us about how we should live out our faith in our own families and communities?

3. In what ways can we be agents of God's renewal in the world today, cultivating justice, peace, and righteousness in our workplaces and social environments?

4. How does the Passover reflect the spiritual battle between good and evil? How can we apply the lessons of faith and obedience in this passage to the spiritual challenges we face in our daily lives?

Exodus 12:31-51

Context and Analysis

Exodus 12:31–51 describes the immediate aftermath of the final plague—the death of the firstborn. Pharaoh, broken and grieving, finally orders the Israelites to leave Egypt (Exod 12:31). This marks the culmination of God's judgment on Egypt and the fulfillment of his promise to deliver Israel. The Israelites, after 430 years in Egypt, are set free to journey toward the land God promised to their forefathers. This passage highlights the institution of the Passover, and the orderly exodus of a large people group signifies both God's power and his faithfulness to his covenant. Pharaoh's response is one of defeat, as he is now forced to submit to the will of God (Exod 12:31). Moses and Aaron act in obedience, leading the people out of Egypt. The Israelites, despite their vulnerability and uncertainty, follow God's command to leave. They depart with confidence in God's protection, shown through the Passover lamb's blood (Exod 12:37). "The LORD kept vigil" (Exod 12:42) indicates God's active protection and provision, as he ensures the safety of his people. The reference to the Passover itself symbolizes divine intervention and the idea of substitutionary atonement (Exod 12:43–50). The idea of God "bringing them out of Egypt" (Exod 12:51) repeats the theme of God's control over history.

Spiritual Insights: Basic Anxiety

The Israelites experience anxiety as they face the unknown. Leaving behind a familiar, though oppressive, life creates uncertainty. Yet, their faith in God's deliverance drives them forward. Pharaoh experiences the ultimate fear of loss—his own son's death—resulting in the collapse of his resolve to resist God. Pharaoh's prior attempts to dominate and control are crushed, revealing his vulnerability. Israelites place their trust in God's provision through the Passover, marking a reliance on divine intervention rather than self-sufficiency (Exod 12:50–51).

Problems and Dilemmas

This passage raises moral and spiritual questions about obedience and leadership. Pharaoh's rebellion against God's command leads to his devastation, while Moses, acting as God's representative, faithfully leads the people out of bondage. The passage emphasizes the contrast between human pride and divine sovereignty. The dilemma for Pharaoh is whether he will continue in rebellion or submit to God, while for the Israelites, it is whether they will trust in God's provision as they leave Egypt.

Themes and Obligations

This passage addresses themes of divine protection (Passover blood) versus human vulnerability (Israelites fleeing with haste). It also raises the responsibility of God's people to obey his commands (Exod 12:50), particularly in observing the Passover, which is to be a perpetual ordinance. The Israelites are tasked with remembering God's deliverance and teaching future generations about his faithfulness (Exod 12:42).

Reflections and Application

This passage speaks to modern struggles with insecurity and fear of the unknown. It demonstrates that trusting in God's sovereignty is the antidote to fear. For modern Christians, the Passover points to Christ as the Lamb who takes away the sins of the world (John 1:29). Like the Israelites, we often set expectations of self-reliance, but God calls us to trust in his timing and provision.

God's Sovereignty and Providence

This section shows God's complete sovereignty over nations and rulers. Pharaoh, once the most powerful figure, is brought to his knees. God's providence is also seen in how he organizes the departure of the Israelites (Exod 12:37).

In the New Testament, we see a similar demonstration of sovereignty in Rom 8:28, where God works all things for the good of those who love him.

Covenant Relationship and Faithfulness

The exodus marks the fulfillment of God's covenant promise to Abraham (Gen 15:13-14). The Passover becomes a symbol of God's faithfulness to his people and a sign of their unique relationship with him. This covenant relationship is mirrored in the New Testament through Christ's sacrifice, which establishes a new covenant (Luke 22:20).

Human Vocation and Cultural Mandate

The Israelites are called to obedience and stewardship of God's commands, including observing the Passover. They are also entrusted with teaching future generations about God's mighty acts (Exod 12:42). In our cultural mandate today, we are called to exercise stewardship over creation and live in obedience to God's commands as part of his mission to renew all things.

Common Grace and Resistance to Evil

This section shows the tension between God's grace toward Israel and his judgment on Egypt. The grace shown to the Israelites in the Passover points to God's common grace that sustains his people, even in the midst of judgment. Christians today are called to resist evil by living out God's grace in the world (Rom 12:21).

God's Grace and Redemptive History

The Passover is a crucial moment in God's redemptive plan, foreshadowing Christ's sacrifice for sin (1 Cor 5:7). Just as the blood of the lamb saved Israel from death, Christ's blood redeems believers from sin and death. This passage calls us to live in light of God's redemptive work and to be agents of his grace in the world.

Questions for Reflection and Discussion

1. How does the Passover in Exod 12 point forward to Christ's work on the cross, and how should this impact our understanding of salvation and grace today?
2. In what ways do we experience fear and anxiety when faced with the unknown, as the Israelites did when leaving Egypt? How can we trust in God's sovereignty in those moments?
3. How does observing God's faithfulness in the past help us remain faithful in our current situations? What responsibilities do we have to teach others about God's faithfulness?
4. How can the story of the exodus challenge us to engage in issues of justice, oppression, and liberty in our world today, as we seek to reflect God's righteousness in our communities?

Cultural Mandate and Kingdom Work

In Exod 12:31–51, the Israelites are finally set free from slavery, marking the beginning of a new chapter in their lives. Though the primary focus of the passage is on the deliverance from Egypt, the underlying principles of the cultural mandate are present. God is preparing his people to fulfill their calling: to cultivate, steward, and develop creation as part of their mission. As they leave Egypt, they begin the journey toward becoming a nation that reflects God's kingdom values, including justice, holiness, and obedience to God's laws.

Application Today: We see that part of our calling is to actively participate in God's mission of renewal, not just spiritually but also in practical ways—cultivating creation, engaging in work that benefits society, and contributing to the common good. As agents of renewal, we are tasked with restoring all things under Christ's lordship (Col 1:20).

Social Mandate and Family Life

Exodus 12:31–51 highlights the corporate nature of Israel's deliverance. Families and communities were central to the observance of the Passover (Exod 12:42–49), and the exodus emphasizes the importance of familial and communal integrity in God's plan. The institution of the Passover points to the importance of teaching God's law and redemptive work to future generations (Exod 12:42), underscoring the role of families in spiritual formation. This passage teaches us that godly families and communities are integral to the advancement of God's purposes. The family is the foundational unit for teaching faith, upholding God's order, and shaping the next generation. Christian communities should support one another in their shared mission, reminding us that faith is not merely individual but communal, grounded in the life of the family and church (Eph 6:4).

Liberty, Justice, and God's Kingdom

Exodus 12:31–51 reveals God's deep concern for justice and liberty as he frees his people from oppression. Pharaoh's oppressive rule over the Israelites is brought to an end by God's judgment, as Pharaoh is forced to release the Israelites (Exod 12:31–33). This deliverance reflects the coming kingdom of God, in which justice will prevail and God's people will experience true freedom (Isa 61:1–3).

Application Today: This section highlights the value of political and economic liberty, grounded in God's righteousness. God does not tolerate the oppression of his people, and his deliverance is both a spiritual and a political liberation. Christians are called to pursue justice today, advocating for liberty and opposing unjust systems that oppress and dehumanize individuals, always grounded in God's righteousness (Mic 6:8). This pursuit of justice reflects the coming kingdom, where God's rule will bring ultimate freedom and peace.

Spiritual Warfare

In this passage, we see the spiritual warfare between God and the powers of Egypt, represented by Pharaoh. God's victory over Egypt's gods (Exod 12:12) shows that spiritual battles are fought not only in the heavens but also on earth, through human decisions and the moral choices of leaders. Pharaoh's continued rebellion against God leads to his downfall, highlighting the consequences of resisting divine authority (Exod 12:31).

Application Today: This passage equips us to stand firm in the face of moral and spiritual challenges. Just as Pharaoh hardened his heart against God, we, too, face temptations to resist God's will. This battle between good and evil plays out in the spiritual and moral decisions we face daily. Christians are called to maintain moral integrity, standing firm in the truth, and resisting evil in all forms (Eph 6:10–12). By trusting in God's sovereignty, we are strengthened to overcome temptation and live faithfully in the face of spiritual warfare.

Questions for Reflection and Discussion

1. How does the exodus of Israel from Egypt serve as a model for how Christians today should view their calling to be agents of renewal in the world? How can we actively participate in God's mission of restoring creation?

2. What role does family play in the life of faith, according to Exod 12:31–51? How can we as individuals and communities prioritize teaching and upholding God's word within our homes and churches?

3. In what ways does God's deliverance of the Israelites inform our understanding of liberty and justice? How can we pursue justice in our own contexts, while remaining grounded in God's righteousness?

4. How can we better equip ourselves to resist evil and maintain moral integrity in the face of spiritual and moral challenges? What lessons from Pharaoh's rebellion and Israel's obedience can we apply to our lives today?

Exodus 13:1–16

Context and Analysis

In Exod 13:1–16, God commands Moses to consecrate every firstborn male—human and animal—as a lasting sign of Israel's deliverance from Egypt. This act is deeply connected to the beginning of the exodus narrative, where Pharaoh sought to destroy Israel's future by ordering the death of all Hebrew baby boys (Exod 1:15–22). In a profound reversal, God not only spares Israel's firstborn during the final plague but also claims them as his own, setting them apart in remembrance of their redemption. The consecration of the firstborn becomes a sacred protest against Pharaoh's brutality and a perpetual reminder that life, freedom, and future belong to God alone. This act of consecration emphasizes God's absolute authority and ownership over his redeemed people. The firstborn represented strength, inheritance, and the security of the family line. Therefore, God's command directly challenges Israel's reliance on human strength and stability, reminding them to place their trust solely in God's providence and care. Historically, consecration served as a powerful reminder of God's sovereign intervention in Israel's deliverance from oppression. It required regular acts of dedication that symbolized the Israelites' dependence upon divine provision rather than their own capabilities or resources.

Spiritual Insights: Human Dependence and Divine Sovereignty

This passage reveals the reality of human dependence upon God for deliverance, provision, and security. God commands the Israelites to continually remember their rescue from Egyptian slavery (Exod 13:3–5), highlighting humanity's tendency to forget past acts of divine grace and instead rely on human wisdom and resources. The redemption and consecration of the firstborn symbolizes God's ultimate authority over all life, underscoring that everything humanity possesses is given and sustained by God alone. The instruction to redeem every firstborn child (Exod 13:13) vividly illustrates human dependence on divine mercy and highlights the necessity of continuous reliance on God rather than human power or control.

Problems and Dilemmas

A critical spiritual tension in this passage is the conflict between human autonomy and willing submission to God's authority. Israel must surrender the instinctive desire for control and self-sufficiency by offering the firstborn to God, symbolizing complete trust and submission. This command tests their obedience, confronting their inclination to maintain control over their possessions and future. This dilemma emphasizes the human tendency toward pride and self-reliance, challenging people to recognize true freedom in submitting to God's sovereign rule. The Israelites' challenge of letting go of their firstborn represents the broader human struggle to relinquish control and trust God's ultimate authority and provision.

Themes and Obligations

The central themes of this passage include God's complete sovereignty, the importance of remembrance, and humanity's ongoing obligation of faithful obedience. The requirement to remember God's deliverance (Exod 13:8–10) establishes memory as crucial for faithful living. Covenant obedience involves not merely acknowledging past acts but actively responding to God's continued grace through practical actions of dedication and trust. The command for Israelites to instruct their children about these rituals (Exod 13:14–16) emphasizes the communal responsibility of faith formation, highlighting that spiritual obligations extend into family life. Teaching future generations ensures the preservation of faith and trust in God's continued faithfulness and provision.

Reflections and Application

This passage addresses contemporary struggles with individualism, self-sufficiency, and the difficulty of surrendering personal resources and future security to God. Like the Israelites who were required to dedicate their firstborn as a sign of reliance, modern believers are similarly called to regularly consecrate their lives, resources, and ambitions to God's service. This passage challenges modern anxieties about security, identity, and purpose, emphasizing that true peace and confidence are found in surrendering control to God's loving authority. Practicing regular acts of dedication and gratitude can cultivate a deeper understanding of humility and dependence upon divine provision rather than human effort or achievement alone.

God's Sovereignty and Providence

Exodus 13:1–16 explicitly portrays God's sovereign authority over Israel's past, present, and future. The redemption and consecration of the firstborn illustrate his meticulous care, reflecting his active role in sustaining and guiding the lives of his people. The institution of rituals like the Feast of Unleavened Bread (Exod 13:6–7) further reminds Israel of God's detailed providence in everyday life, as well as his overarching control of history. The passage encourages believers today to trust deeply in God's sovereignty in both major decisions and ordinary circumstances, recognizing that God's purposes are ultimately good, even when his ways may appear challenging or unclear from a human perspective.

Covenant Relationship and Faithfulness

This passage underscores the covenant relationship between God and his people, highlighting that the Israelites' consecration of the firstborn is rooted in their identity as a redeemed community. The Israelites respond to God's prior acts of redemption with obedient gratitude, fulfilling their covenant responsibilities through practical acts of dedication and remembrance. This passage challenges contemporary believers to faithfully fulfill their covenant responsibilities, grounded in gratitude for God's grace and deliverance. The Israelites' ongoing dedication symbolizes the lifelong commitment believers are called to maintain, consistently trusting God's promises and faithfully responding to his gracious actions in history. In Exod 13:1–16, we see the foundational role of memory and consecration in fulfilling the cultural mandate, which calls humans to steward and cultivate creation under God's authority. The consecration of the firstborn (Exod 13:2) serves as a recognition that all life belongs to God, and humans are to live in obedience to his purposes. The command to observe this ritual as a perpetual ordinance (Exod 13:10) ensures that Israel would remember God's redemptive work throughout generations, embedding stewardship of God's story into the fabric of daily life.

Application Today: We can apply this in our work and engagement by remembering that all we do is under God's sovereignty. Whether in our careers, families, or community service, we are agents of God's kingdom, called to renew and restore creation by upholding the values of righteousness, justice, and grace. This section reminds us that all our work must be consecrated to God as we participate in his mission to redeem and restore the world (Col 3:17).

Social Mandate and Family Life

The instruction to tell the next generation about the significance of consecrating the firstborn (Exod 13:8) emphasizes the family's role in teaching the faith. This passage underscores the importance of strong family structures for passing on the covenantal relationship between God and his people. The act of consecration is a communal and family-centered one, reminding parents of their responsibility to instruct their children in the ways of the Lord, integrating faith into the daily rhythms of life (Exod 13:14).

Application Today: In today's society, where individualism often overshadows communal responsibility, this passage challenges us to see the family as the primary context for faith formation. As parents and guardians, we must take up the responsibility of teaching our children about God's work and mission, ensuring that faith is central in our homes (Eph 6:4). Communities and churches can also support families in this critical task.

Liberty, Justice, and God's Kingdom

The liberation of Israel from Egypt (which this chapter calls them to remember) reflects God's concern for justice and freedom. God's act of deliverance is both political and economic, as he frees his people from slavery and oppressive structures (Exod 13:3). By commemorating this event through the consecration of the firstborn, Israel is reminded that their liberty is rooted in God's justice, not in human power. It is God's righteousness that secures their freedom and requires them to live justly as his covenant people.

Application Today: For Christians, this passage points to the ongoing pursuit of justice and liberty grounded in God's righteousness. This pursuit is not only personal but also societal, as we are called to challenge unjust systems, seek the flourishing of all people, and advocate for liberty that reflects God's kingdom values (Matt 5–7; Luke 4:18–19). Justice flows from the character of God and must be a core commitment of God's people in both its political and economic engagement with the world.

Spiritual Warfare

This section, with its focus on remembering God's deliverance, also serves as a call to moral integrity and vigilance. Israel is commanded to consecrate their firstborn as a sign of their ongoing reliance on God's power and protection (Exod 13:12–13). This act of consecration not only marks them as God's people but also sets them apart from the nations around them. The instruction to observe these practices serves as a spiritual safeguard against forgetfulness, complacency, and moral decline.

Application Today: In a world where spiritual and moral challenges abound, this passage calls believers to stand firm in their identity as God's people. By consecrating ourselves to God—both in our daily actions and in our moral decisions—we resist the forces of evil and maintain our witness to the world. Life is a battleground for God's kingdom, and we are called to live with integrity, standing firm in the face of temptations and moral challenges (Eph 6:10–12).

Questions for Reflection and Discussion

1. How does the consecration of the firstborn in this chapter remind us of God's claim on all aspects of life? In what ways can we apply the idea of consecration to our daily work and responsibilities?

2. This section emphasizes the importance of passing down the story of God's deliverance to the next generation. How can we, in our families or communities, create practices of remembrance that teach future generations about God's faithfulness?

3. What does this passage teach us about justice and freedom, particularly in light of God's deliverance of Israel from Egypt? How can we pursue liberty and justice in our society today, reflecting God's righteousness?

4. How does the act of consecration challenge us to live with moral integrity and stand firm against the spiritual and moral challenges of our time? How can we, as individuals and as a community, maintain our witness in a world that often opposes God's values?

Exodus 13:17—14:31

Context and Analysis

In this passage, the Israelites are finally leaving Egypt, but God does not lead them along the most direct path. Instead, they are directed toward the Red Sea (Exod 13:17–18), illustrating God's sovereign control over the journey. Historically, Egypt had great military power, and Pharaoh viewed the Israelites as an economic asset. When the Egyptians pursued them (Exod 14:5–9), it placed Israel in a position of extreme vulnerability. Key themes include fear, vulnerability, and divine intervention. The Israelites initially respond with fear, questioning Moses (Exod 14:11–12), but Moses assures them that God will deliver them. The phrase "The Lord will fight for you" (Exod 14:14) underscores divine intervention, and the miraculous parting of the Red Sea (Exod 14:21) symbolizes God's sovereignty over creation and his protection of his covenant people.

Spiritual Insights: Basic Anxiety

The Israelites experience anxiety and fear due to their vulnerability. With the Egyptians pursuing them and the sea before them, their helplessness is clear (Exod 14:10). Their reaction includes despair and accusations toward Moses (Exod 14:11–12), indicating their lack of trust in God. Moses's response is a call to trust in God, who is sovereign over their circumstances. The Israelites are called to stand firm and witness God's salvation (Exod 14:13–14). This passage highlights a struggle between relying on oneself versus trusting in God. Their anxiety gives way to trust and obedience once God intervenes (Exod 14:31).

Problems and Dilemmas

The spiritual dilemma here centers on faith and obedience. The Israelites' fear and doubt lead them to question God's plan and Moses's leadership. This reveals a tension between their real, understandable fear and the idealized trust they are called to exhibit. Their fear exposes their struggle to obey God in the face of overwhelming danger. Moses reminds them that God alone will bring deliverance, but the dilemma underscores human fragility in times of crisis. Obedience and faith become critical themes when facing overwhelming challenges, and the passage illustrates the gap between the Israelites' fear and God's faithfulness.

Themes and Obligations

This passage addresses the theme of God's protection versus human vulnerability. The Israelites are powerless against the Egyptian army, but God demonstrates his might by parting the Red Sea (Exod 14:21–22). Their reliance on God's intervention becomes a profound lesson in trust and submission. God's actions call his people to recognize that their deliverance is entirely dependent on his power. The Israelites' response to God's deliverance is one of awe and faith (Exod 14:31), revealing that their ethical and spiritual obligation is to trust in God's provision, not in human strength.

Reflections and Application

This passage speaks to modern struggles with insecurity, fear of failure, and anxiety about the future. Just as the Israelites were caught between the Egyptian army and the sea, we often find ourselves in seemingly impossible situations. Their response—initial fear, then trust in God's deliverance—mirrors our own challenges in faith. The concept of the idealized self is relevant here. The Israelites had unrealistic expectations of their journey, which led to frustration when they faced hardships. Similarly, we may have false expectations of how life should go, leading to anxiety when things don't meet our ideals. This passage reminds us that God's plan is often different from our own, and trusting in him leads to ultimate deliverance, even in difficult circumstances.

God's Sovereignty and Providence

This passage powerfully reveals God's sovereignty and providence. By leading the Israelites in a way that seemed counterintuitive, God was positioning them for a miraculous deliverance (Exod 14:3-4). The parting of the Red Sea demonstrates God's authority over nature and history, showing that he is in control even when circumstances seem dire. This passage challenges us to recognize God's authority in both personal and societal leadership. It teaches us to trust that God's plans are always for his glory and our good, even when we cannot see the full picture (Rom 8:28).

Covenant Relationship and Faithfulness

The covenant relationship between God and Israel is on display as God acts decisively to protect and deliver his chosen people. God's faithfulness to his covenant is demonstrated through his mighty deeds (Exod 14:21-22). This passage encourages us to live out our covenant obligations, trusting in God's provision and faithfulness even in the face of fear and doubt. The Israelites' ultimate recognition of God's power and faithfulness (Exod 14:31) serves as a reminder for us to trust in God's covenant promises in our own lives.

Human Vocation and Cultural Mandate

Although this passage is primarily about deliverance, it also points to the larger role Israel will play in God's redemptive plan. God delivers Israel, not just to free them from slavery but to establish them as his chosen nation—a people through whom he will bless the world (Gen 12:2-3). Their vocation is to be a light to the nations, modeling obedience and trust in God. For believers today, this points to our calling to serve as agents of renewal, stewarding creation and participating in God's mission to restore all things (Matt 28:19-20). Our vocation involves trusting in God's sovereignty as we engage in his kingdom work.

Common Grace and Resistance to Evil

This passage highlights the tension between good and evil as represented by Pharaoh's relentless pursuit of Israel (Exod 14:5-9). Pharaoh represents the forces of evil and oppression, while God's deliverance represents his grace and protection over his people. God's intervention shows his grace at work in preserving his people from destruction. The passage challenges us to resist evil, knowing that God's grace is greater and that all good gifts come from him (Jas 1:17). Even when evil seems overpowering, God's grace sustains and delivers his people.

God's Grace and Redemptive History

Exodus 14 is a pivotal moment in redemptive history. The parting of the Red Sea prefigures later acts of deliverance, most notably Christ's work on the cross. The Israelites' rescue from slavery foreshadows the greater rescue that Christ provides from sin and death (1 Cor 10:1–2). This section reminds us that God's grace has been at work throughout history, moving toward the ultimate redemption of his people. We can apply this understanding by recognizing that God's grace shapes all of history, and our lives are part of that larger redemptive plan. As we engage with the world, we do so knowing that God's redemptive work continues, and we are participants in his kingdom mission.

Cultural Mandate and Kingdom Work

In Exod 13:17—14:31, God leads Israel out of Egypt, but not by the shortest route through the Philistine country, because they might face war and return to Egypt (Exod 13:17). Instead, he leads them toward the Red Sea, demonstrating that God is not only concerned with the immediate need for liberation but also with the preservation and flourishing of his people. This passage highlights God's sovereignty over creation and his ongoing involvement in guiding and protecting his people, aligning with the cultural mandate to cultivate and steward creation responsibly (Gen 1:28). The miraculous parting of the Red Sea (Exod 14:21) shows God's control over nature, reinforcing the mandate to be agents of renewal in both work and rest. As God's people today, we can engage in our work, recognizing that God's mission includes the restoration of all things through Christ (Col 1:20).

Social Mandate and Family Life

In this chapter, family and community dynamics are critical as God instructs Moses to gather all of Israel and lead them out of bondage (Exod 13:18). God commands them to take Joseph's bones (Exod 13:19), showing respect for the ancestors and emphasizing continuity in the family of God.

The protection and deliverance of the entire nation—families, women, children—underscores the importance of strong families and communities in God's covenant plan. This passage reinforces the idea that the family unit is central to the advancement of God's purposes. God's deliverance of Israel teaches us the importance of social order rooted in godly families and communities. Just as God protected and guided Israel, we are to uphold God's order in our families today, fostering godly relationships and supporting one another in faith (Deut 6:6–9).

Liberty, Justice, and God's Kingdom

Exodus 13:17—14:31 presents a powerful image of God's justice and liberation. The Israelites are freed from centuries of slavery in Egypt, demonstrating God's concern for liberty and justice. The destruction of Pharaoh's army in the Red Sea (Exod 14:28) underscores God's commitment to freeing his people from oppression and tyranny. This section speaks to the divine origin of liberty, showing that freedom is rooted in God's righteousness. The Israelites did not achieve freedom through their own efforts but by trusting in God's deliverance. Today, we are called to pursue justice and liberty that reflects God's kingdom, advocating for freedom from oppression and maintaining justice in our societies, knowing that true freedom comes from submission to God's reign (2 Cor 3:17).

Spiritual Warfare

The crossing of the Red Sea and the confrontation between Pharaoh's army and the Israelites is a vivid example of spiritual warfare (Exod 14:13–14). The Israelites face overwhelming odds and fear, but Moses encourages them to trust in God's deliverance: "The LORD will fight for you; you need only to be still" (Exod 14:14). This reinforces the spiritual principle that God fights on behalf of his people, even when circumstances seem impossible. This passage teaches us that spiritual warfare is often about standing firm in faith and trusting in God's power. The destruction of Pharaoh's army (Exod 14:27–28) also highlights the moral dimension of trusting God rather than relying on human strength. Today, we face spiritual and moral challenges, but this chapter equips us to stand firm, knowing that God is fighting our battles (Eph 6:12–13). We are called to live with integrity, trusting in God's sovereign power over evil.

Questions for Reflection and Discussion

1. In what ways do you identify with the Israelites' experience of fear and anxiety when faced with overwhelming or uncertain circumstances? How can Moses's call to stand firm and trust in God's deliverance encourage you in specific struggles you are currently facing?

2. How does the Israelites' unexpected journey and miraculous crossing of the Red Sea affect your understanding of God's sovereignty, especially when your own plans and expectations do not unfold as anticipated? In what ways can you grow in trusting God's timing and guidance?

3. Reflecting on the Israelites' deliverance from oppression, how does this passage instruct us as Christians to engage with issues of injustice and evil in today's world? What are practical steps we can take to actively resist injustice while placing our ultimate trust in God's grace and victory?

4. The entire Israelite community, including families, experienced deliverance together. How does this highlight the significance of covenant community and family life in advancing God's purposes? In what ways can we strengthen and support godly family and community relationships in our contexts today?

Exodus 15:1–21

Context and Analysis

Exodus 15:1–21 is known as "The Song of the Sea," a hymn of praise and thanksgiving that Moses and the Israelites sing after God delivers them from the Egyptians by parting the Red Sea. The historical context involves Israel's miraculous escape from Egypt and the drowning of Pharaoh's army (Exod 14:27–28). This passage is a moment of triumph after the years of oppression and the tension of the Red Sea encounter. The song praises God's power, divine intervention, and faithfulness. Repeated phrases like "The Lord is my strength and my defense" (Exod 15:2) and "The Lord reigns for ever and ever" (Exod 15:18) highlight themes of God's absolute sovereignty and the fear and awe he inspires among the nations. The song contrasts Israel's vulnerability with God's omnipotence, showing how the Israelites respond to their fear and dependence on God with worship.

Spiritual Insights: Basic Anxiety

Before the miracle at the Red Sea, the Israelites faced profound anxiety. They had been trapped between the advancing Egyptian army and the Red Sea (Exod 14:10–12). In Exod 15, their response to anxiety is transformed into praise. Their feelings of fear and helplessness are alleviated not through self-expansion or control but through God's intervention. The Israelites trusted God instead of their own strength, as symbolized by their worship of God's victory in the song. They express a form of submission and reliance on divine protection. When they sing, "The Lord is a warrior; the Lord is his name" (Exod 15:3), they acknowledge that their deliverance comes not from human power but from God's sovereignty. This teaches us the importance of placing trust in God in the face of fear and insecurity (cf. Phil 4:6–7).

Problems and Dilemmas

One key dilemma is the contrast between Israel's vulnerability and God's overwhelming power. Before the Red Sea event, Israel had questioned their decision to leave Egypt. They were tempted to return to a life of slavery for the sake of perceived safety (Exod 14:11–12). The song in Exod 15 resolves this tension by highlighting the absolute futility of relying on anything or anyone other than God. This passage challenges readers to trust God in moments when faith is difficult. The idealized self would want control over situations, but the real self acknowledges dependence on God. The deeper conflict is whether Israel can maintain faith in God's promise after seeing his power displayed. We are similarly challenged in our own lives to obey and trust, even in times of uncertainty (cf. Heb 11:29).

Themes and Obligations

The passage addresses God's protection and the obligation to respond to his faithfulness. The repeated praise of God's strength and the destruction of the Egyptians (Exod 15:4–7) reminds us of the human vulnerability to sin and evil but also of divine provision and grace. The Israelites' praise is their acknowledgment of their duty to worship God in response to his deliverance. This text places moral and ethical responsibilities on God's people. Israel's response to God's victory serves as a model for how believers are to respond to God's faithfulness—with praise, gratitude, and trust. Just as Israel recognized God's leadership and kingship (Exod 15:18), we are called to acknowledge God's authority over our lives and trust in his continued guidance (cf. Col 1:13–14).

Reflections and Application

This passage speaks powerfully to modern struggles with fear and insecurity. Like Israel, we often face moments where we feel trapped or helpless. The Israelites' song encourages us to place our faith in God, knowing that he is powerful and faithful to deliver. Today, we may wrestle with unrealistic expectations of ourselves or perfectionism in our spiritual lives, but this passage reminds us that our hope lies in God's action, not our own efforts.

Today, this passage speaks to contexts of leadership, community challenges, and personal struggles with identity and purpose. Whether in leadership positions, personal fears, or challenges, this chapter invites us to respond with worship and trust rather than self-reliance. Leaders and communities can benefit from learning to trust in God's power and providence rather than their abilities.

God's Sovereignty and Providence

This section demonstrates God's sovereignty by displaying his control over creation and the forces of nature, such as the parting of the Red Sea (Exod 14:21) and the destruction of the Egyptian forces (Exod 15:4–5). The Israelites' response to this divine act emphasizes God's ultimate authority and providence in the world, which should encourage us to submit fully to his will in every aspect of our lives. The praise in verses 11–12 ("Who among the gods is like you, Lord? Who is like you—majestic in holiness, awesome in glory, working wonders?") reflects God's transcendent majesty. Today, believers are reminded of God's authority not only over personal matters but also over global and societal issues, challenging us to trust his sovereign control (cf. Rom 8:28).

Covenant Relationship and Faithfulness

The song in Exod 15 reflects the covenant relationship between God and his people. God's deliverance is an act of covenant faithfulness to the promises made to Abraham, Isaac, and Jacob. The Israelites' praise of God for keeping his promises reminds us of our obligations to live faithfully before him, recognizing that his grace sustains us. Just as Israel trusted God's deliverance, we must trust in his faithfulness (cf. 2 Cor 1:20).

Human Vocation and Cultural Mandate

Though this passage focuses on worship and deliverance, it indirectly highlights the Israelites' role in God's larger plan. They were delivered for a purpose—to become a people who worship and serve God in the land promised to them (Exod 15:13). Similarly, believers today are called to engage in the world, participating in God's mission of renewal, whether through work, rest, or acts of service, recognizing that all is done under his providence.

Common Grace and Resistance to Evil

This passage displays a dramatic tension between good and evil, with Pharaoh's forces representing oppressive evil and God representing divine justice. God's grace preserves and protects his people, even when they were helpless, while simultaneously executing judgment on their oppressors (Exod 15:6–7). This section calls us to recognize evil in the world, resist it, and trust in God's ultimate justice. We can also see God's grace at work in preserving and sustaining society, despite evil's presence (cf. Matt 5:45).

God's Grace and Redemptive History

The crossing of the Red Sea and the subsequent song of deliverance is a pivotal moment in redemptive history, showing God's grace in delivering his people from bondage. This act of grace points forward to the greater deliverance that comes through Jesus Christ, who leads his people out of the bondage of sin (cf. Rom 6:22). Just as God redeemed Israel, Christ redeems his church. This section challenges us to live in light of that redemption, engaging in societal and cultural issues as agents of God's kingdom.

Questions for Reflection and Discussion

1. How does God's deliverance of Israel in this passage reflect his covenant faithfulness? How can we trust in God's faithfulness in our own lives today?
2. The Israelites faced overwhelming fear at the Red Sea. What fears or insecurities are you facing today, and how can this passage encourage you to trust God?
3. How does this passage teach us about God's justice and sovereignty over evil? What does this mean for how we approach issues of justice in our world today?
4. How does this passage inspire us to respond to God's deliverance with worship? How can we make worship and gratitude central to our daily lives?

Cultural Mandate and Kingdom Work

In Exod 15:1–21, the Israelites sing a song of victory after God delivered them from Egypt by parting the Red Sea. This passage shows how God's people are to respond to his work in creation, recognizing his sovereignty over all things. While the immediate focus is on God's triumph over Egypt, the broader theological significance points to God's rule over creation and human history. The cultural mandate (Gen 1:28) to cultivate and steward creation is reflected in the idea that God's people are called to recognize his authority in all aspects of life. Here, Israel acknowledges God as the sovereign ruler of the earth (Exod 15:18, "The LORD reigns for ever and ever"). This can be applied to our modern engagement in the world by participating in God's redemptive work—whether in our vocations, family life, or community—in recognition of his overarching kingdom. The text informs our calling to be agents of renewal by showing that God's victory over oppression is not just a past event but part of an ongoing mission to restore creation. By aligning our work with God's purposes, we participate in his kingdom work today (Col 3:23–24).

Social Mandate and Family Life

Exodus 15 underscores the importance of communal worship and familial participation in praising God for his deliverance. As Miriam, Aaron's sister, leads the women in song and dance (Exod 15:20), the communal aspect of worship is highlighted, drawing in families and communities. This passage reminds us of the need for godly families and communities to actively remember and celebrate God's faithfulness. Families are not just passive recipients of God's grace but active participants in responding to his works. In today's context, this can apply to how families and local communities foster faith through communal worship, service, and discipleship, thereby advancing God's purposes in society. By maintaining a biblical social order in families and communities, we follow God's design for human flourishing and contribute to the advancement of his kingdom on earth (cf. Eph 6:4).

Liberty, Justice, and God's Kingdom

This section is a profound celebration of God's deliverance from political oppression and injustice. God's defeat of the Egyptian forces represents his intervention for liberty and justice on behalf of his people. By parting the Red Sea, God destroys Israel's oppressors and leads them toward freedom, reflecting his concern for political and economic liberty (Exod 15:13, "In your unfailing love you will lead the people you have redeemed"). Grounded in God's righteousness, this passage highlights the importance of resisting tyranny and recognizing God's role as the ultimate liberator. The pursuit of justice in this context is not merely political, but deeply theological—God intervenes to free his people from slavery and lead them to live as his covenant community. This informs our engagement with justice today, encouraging believers to reflect God's justice by advocating for political and economic liberty in ways that honor his kingdom principles (cf. Gal 5:1).

Spiritual Warfare

Exodus 15 vividly portrays the spiritual battle between God and the oppressive forces of Egypt. God is described as a warrior (Exod 15:3, "The LORD is a warrior"), emphasizing his direct involvement in the fight against evil. The victory over Egypt is not just political but spiritual, demonstrating that God is committed to defending his people from those who seek to enslave them. This passage offers a model for understanding spiritual warfare in the Christian life. Just as God fought for Israel, he fights for his people today in the spiritual realm. The moral integrity of God's people is maintained by their recognition of his power and their dependence on his deliverance. The song of victory reminds believers that the battle belongs to the LORD, and that trusting in him is key to overcoming moral and spiritual challenges (cf. Eph 6:10–18).

Questions for Reflection and Discussion

1. How does recognizing God's victory over Egypt shape the way we approach our own work and engagement in the world today? How can we be agents of renewal in our work and rest, participating in God's mission?

2. How can we incorporate the communal worship seen in Exod 15 into our family life and church communities today? How do we ensure that we are passing down the remembrance of God's faithfulness to the next generation?

3. What does this passage teach us about God's concern for political and economic liberty? How can we as Christians engage in promoting justice and liberty in today's world in ways that reflect God's righteousness?

4. In what ways does Exod 15 remind us of the spiritual battles we face today? How can we maintain moral integrity and trust God in the face of challenges that seem beyond our control? How do we apply the concept that "The LORD is a warrior" in our own spiritual lives today?

Exodus 15:22—16:36

Context and Analysis

In Exod 15:22—16:36, the Israelites begin their journey through the wilderness after their miraculous deliverance at the Red Sea. Their initial joy turns quickly to grumbling as they encounter bitter water at Marah (Exod 15:23), hunger in the Desert of Sin (Exod 16:2-3), and uncertainty about their survival. This section highlights how God's people, though rescued from bondage, are still learning what it means to live in daily dependence on his provision. Key themes include divine provision, human complaint, and the discipline of obedience. The LORD responds to the people's need not by rebuking them, but by graciously providing water, manna, and quail—accompanied by specific commands (Exod 16:4-5, 16-26). These moments are not only responses to physical needs but opportunities to form the people morally and spiritually through patterns of dependence and trust.

Spiritual Insights: Basic Anxiety and the Search for Security

Karen Horney's theory of basic anxiety—a deep sense of helplessness and fear in a world perceived as unpredictable or hostile—offers a compelling lens through which to view the Israelites' behavior in this passage. Having just experienced God's powerful deliverance at the Red Sea, they are now thrust into the unknown wilderness, a place where basic needs like water and food are uncertain. This abrupt transition from the structured familiarity of Egypt to the uncertainty of freedom provokes a crisis of emotional security. The Israelites' grumbling at Marah and in the Desert of Sin can be seen as expressions of basic anxiety. Deprived of stability, they begin to display anxiety-driven responses. Their complaints reflect a desire to regain some sense of control, even romanticizing slavery as preferable to present uncertainty (Exod 16:3). These are classic symptoms of the inner conflict Horney described—responses to a loss of safety that can include blaming others, expressing hostility, or retreating into idealized past conditions. Rather than punishing this anxiety, God provides structure: daily manna, strict instructions, and the Sabbath rest. In Horneyan terms, this is a therapeutic response to neurotic anxiety—offering security through consistent, dependable provision. God does not just meet their physical needs; he provides a pattern of life that restores internal stability and teaches them to trust, obey, and rest. The wilderness becomes a place where their emotional and spiritual maturity is gently formed through rhythms that counter fear with faithfulness.

Problems and Dilemmas

The spiritual dilemma here centers on trust versus control. The Israelites' grumbling reveals a fear-driven desire for autonomy, a longing to return to the predictability of Egypt—even if it meant oppression—rather than walk in the vulnerability of freedom under God's care (Exod 16:3). This reflects the broader human struggle: preferring the illusion of self-sufficiency over the discomfort of trust. The challenge is not merely about physical hunger but about spiritual formation. God's testing (Exod 16:4) is not punitive but purposeful, inviting the people to grow in faith. The real issue is whether the Israelites will learn to submit to God's order in even the smallest of daily matters—what to gather, how much, and when to rest.

Themes and Obligations

Themes of providence, discipline, and covenant responsibility permeate this section. God's provision of manna and quail is an act of mercy, but it is not unconditional. Obedience is required. The instructions around gathering and resting teach the people that trust in God must shape every aspect of life, including labor and rest. There is also a communal obligation here: every household gathers what is needed—not too much, not too little—and all are sustained together (Exod 16:17–18). This pattern points to an ethic of mutual care, contentment, and justice. In learning to depend on God, the people also learn to live responsibly with one another.

Reflections and Application

This passage speaks to the modern condition of anxiety, restlessness, and the temptation to rely on human strategies for security. Like the Israelites, we are often tempted to believe that freedom from difficulty means the absence of dependency. But God uses need, scarcity, and uncertainty to reorient our desires and teach us to live by grace. The Israelites' yearning for Egypt reminds us of how easily we idealize former securities, even when they enslaved us. This passage invites us to resist the illusion of control and embrace a life of rhythm and trust. The Sabbath command embedded in the manna story is especially relevant: it teaches that God's provision is sufficient and that rest is not a luxury, but a response of faith.

God's Sovereignty and Providence

The entire structure of this passage reflects the sovereignty of God over creation and over time. From bitter water made sweet (Exod 15:25) to bread from heaven (Exod 16:4), every detail points to God's intimate governance of his people's lives. The daily appearance of manna, its impermanence, and its double portion on the sixth day demonstrate that even nature itself obeys God's sustaining word. This passage challenges us to live with an awareness that God's rule is not abstract, but present in the details of our days—in when we rise, when we work, what we eat, and when we rest. God's care is constant, and his timing and instructions are always for our good, even when they test our preferences.

Covenant Relationship and Faithfulness

The provision of manna and the instructions that accompany it are not random acts of kindness; they are covenantal. God is not only feeding his people but shaping them to be his own—a people who live in daily dependence, who rest in his sufficiency, and who bear witness to his faithfulness in how they order their lives. This passage calls us to remember that our lives are not our own. We belong to a God who redeems, provides, and forms us. Our obedience is not a burden, but a response to grace. In learning to live with less, trust more, and rest regularly, we reflect a deeper reality: we are not sustained by our own strength, but by the faithful hand of God.

Cultural Mandate and Kingdom Work

In Exod 15:22—16:36, the cultural mandate is reflected in the way God sustains his people and teaches them to steward the creation around them. After leading the Israelites into the wilderness, God provides water from a bitter source at Marah (Exod 15:23-25) and then manna and quail to meet their daily needs (Exod 16:4-15). This provision demonstrates that God continues to uphold his creation, even in the desolation of the wilderness. In the context of work and rest, the chapter emphasizes the importance of gathering manna daily, with specific instructions to gather twice as much before the Sabbath, showing God's design for both labor and rest (Exod 16:22-26). This balance speaks to our ongoing cultural mandate to cultivate the earth and steward its resources while also recognizing the limits God places on our work to allow for rest and worship.

Application Today: Christians are called to work diligently in their vocations, trusting in God's provision and participating in his mission to restore creation. This means being faithful in both our daily work and in the call to rest, recognizing that both work and rest are acts of faith in God's sustaining power (Col 3:23-24).

Social Mandate and Family Life

This passage also teaches us about the social and family dynamics of God's people. The instructions for gathering manna are directed toward families, with each family gathering as much as they needed (Exod 16:16). This distribution system, rooted in God's provision, reflects the social structure of the Israelite community, where families are responsible for each other's well-being. Moreover, the concept of the Sabbath as a day of rest (Exod 16:23-30) extends beyond individual practice to encompass the entire community. The family unit plays a crucial role in honoring this commandment, and it underscores the importance of godly order within family and society. By observing the Sabbath, families together acknowledge God's rule and provision, fostering communal worship and reinforcing their covenant relationship with God.

Application Today: Families and communities are integral to advancing God's purposes. We are called to lead our families in the ways of the Lord, ensuring that we not only care for physical needs but also prioritize spiritual practices like Sabbath rest. This contributes to the flourishing of both individual families and the broader community of faith.

Liberty, Justice, and God's Kingdom

The provision of manna in the wilderness (Exod 16:4-15) speaks to God's justice and care for his people. He frees them from the bondage of Egypt and provides for them in the desert, demonstrating his concern for both their spiritual and physical liberty. This act of provision reflects God's righteousness, showing that true freedom is found in dependence on him, rather than on human systems or power. In a broader sense, the passage highlights the necessity of relying on God for sustenance rather than falling back into the "security" of slavery in Egypt (Exod 16:3). God's kingdom justice involves freeing people from both physical and spiritual bondage, and this justice calls his people to live in liberty, grounded in trust and obedience to his word.

Application Today: Christians are called to pursue justice and liberty, recognizing that true freedom comes from God. Our role is to resist systems of oppression—whether personal, political, or economic—by trusting in God's provision and advocating for justice in a way that reflects the coming kingdom of God (Luke 4:18).

Spiritual Warfare

In Exod 16, the Israelites face the spiritual challenge of trusting in God's provision versus relying on their own understanding. Despite witnessing God's miracles, they struggle with doubt and grumble against Moses and Aaron (Exod 16:2). Their testing of God's commands—such as gathering manna on the Sabbath despite his instructions not to (Exod 16:27)—highlights the ongoing spiritual battle between obedience and disobedience. This passage emphasizes the moral integrity required to follow God's commands, especially when circumstances seem uncertain. The manna test (Exod 16:4) is a spiritual test of trust and discipline, requiring the Israelites to obey God daily. Spiritual warfare in this context is about resisting the temptation to doubt God's provision and to live by faith in his word.

Application Today: Believers face similar spiritual challenges in trusting God in difficult times. This passage reminds us of the importance of moral integrity and faithfulness to God's word, even when it feels counterintuitive. It equips us to stand firm in our faith, knowing that God is our provider and sustainer in all circumstances (Eph 6:10-17).

Questions for Reflection and Discussion

1. The Israelites struggled with trusting God for their daily needs. How do you struggle with trusting God in uncertain times, and how can this passage challenge us to surrender control?

2. What does this passage teach us about the balance between work and rest? How can we better practice Sabbath rest in a society that values constant productivity?

3. The Israelites tested God by gathering manna on the Sabbath, despite his instructions. In what areas of life do we tend to test God's instructions, and how can we cultivate deeper obedience?

4. God provides for the Israelites in the wilderness, freeing them from both physical hunger and spiritual anxiety. How can we pursue justice and liberty in our communities while trusting in God's provision for both spiritual and physical needs?

Exodus 17

Context and Analysis

In Exod 17, the Israelites continue their journey through the wilderness and encounter two major challenges. First, they face a physical crisis at Rephidim: there is no water, and the people begin to quarrel with Moses (Exod 17:1–7). Their grumbling escalates to the point where Moses fears for his life (Exod 17:4). In response, God miraculously provides water from a rock, demonstrating his ongoing provision and presence. The second half of the chapter recounts Israel's battle against Amalek (Exod 17:8–16). Joshua leads the army while Moses, with Aaron and Hur's support, raises his hands in intercession. As long as Moses's hands are raised, Israel prevails. This scene vividly illustrates the connection between human effort, spiritual dependence, and divine intervention. Key themes in this chapter include testing, interdependence, leadership, and God's covenantal faithfulness. Both episodes reflect Israel's ongoing formation as a people who must trust not only in God's provision, but in the structure of leadership and community that God has placed around them.

Spiritual Insights: Basic Anxiety and Conflict

Karen Horney's concept of basic anxiety—a deep, persistent sense of helplessness and insecurity—provides a compelling framework for understanding the Israelites' reaction in this passage. After repeated experiences of God's faithfulness, the people still respond to adversity not with trust, but with accusation and panic. Their demand for water (Exod 17:2) and the escalating hostility toward Moses (Exod 17:3–4) suggest a community overwhelmed by anxiety about survival and stability. Horney observed that people often develop neurotic coping strategies in response to anxiety: moving toward others (seeking reassurance), moving against others (expressing hostility and control), or moving away (emotional withdrawal). In Exod 17:1–7, we see a movement against—the people project their fear onto Moses and demand immediate solutions, even threatening violence. Their anxiety blinds them to the memory of God's past provisions. Rather than condemning their fear, God meets their anxiety with reassurance through a miraculous act. Water from the rock not only quenches physical thirst but signals that God remains present, attentive, and faithful. This grace under pressure speaks to God's willingness to stabilize his people emotionally and spiritually when they spiral into fear. In the second half of the chapter, the battle with Amalek provides a striking counter-image: Moses, Aaron, and Hur model mutual support and interdependence in the face of external threat. Rather than reacting out of anxiety, they embody a mature response—trusting in God while standing firm together. This contrast highlights the growth that begins to emerge when God's people learn to process their fears through faith, shared responsibility, and perseverance.

Problems and Dilemmas

The central dilemma in this chapter is again one of trust versus fear. The people question, "Is the LORD among us or not?" (Exod 17:7), revealing their spiritual amnesia and emotional fragility. Their anxiety leads them to project blame rather than remember grace. Moses himself is caught in the middle, both leader and target. The battle with Amalek introduces a different kind of dilemma: the tension between human agency and divine sovereignty. Victory depends on Joshua's leadership, the army's strength, and Moses's intercession—yet all are undergirded by God's power. The scene reveals how faith requires, not passive waiting but coordinated trust, humility, and action.

Themes and Obligations

This section reinforces the themes of divine provision, human dependence, communal responsibility, and spiritual formation. God continues to provide in response to need, but also through relational structures. Moses needs Aaron and Hur; Joshua needs Moses's intercession; the people need leadership. None can thrive alone. There is also a strong obligation to remember: the naming of the place as Massah and Meribah (Exod 17:7) serves as a warning against future forgetfulness. Likewise, God commands

Moses to record the victory over Amalek as a memorial (Exod 17:14), reinforcing the ethical obligation to remember both God's provision and the human partnerships that sustained them.

Reflections and Application

This passage speaks directly to today's experiences of anxiety, blame, and disconnection. In times of crisis, we often mirror the Israelites—lashing out at others or doubting God's presence. The temptation to "move against" others can damage relationships and blind us to God's ongoing work in our lives. But the battle scene offers a redemptive picture of what faithful response looks like: humility, shared burden, and intercession. We are not meant to face our battles alone. In families, churches, and communities, God calls us to lift one another's arms when we grow tired, to fight together rather than fracture under stress.

God's Sovereignty and Providence

God's sovereignty is revealed in both his provision of water and his orchestration of Israel's military victory. In the face of basic needs and life-threatening enemies, God is neither absent nor indifferent. His care reaches into the most physical and practical aspects of life—quenching thirst, ensuring victory, preserving leadership. This passage reminds us that God's rule encompasses both the ordinary and the extraordinary. Whether through striking a rock or raising hands in prayer, God invites us to trust him fully—not only in crisis, but in the daily rhythms of responsibility and cooperation.

Covenant Relationship and Faithfulness

Exodus 17 continues to develop Israel's covenant identity. The people must learn not only to trust in God's power but to live in accordance with his design for communal life. Moses's leadership, Aaron and Hur's support, and Joshua's military role each contribute to a whole that reflects God's covenantal order. The people's failure to trust becomes a lesson, while their eventual triumph is meant to be remembered. Trust and obedience are not abstract ideals; they are enacted through faith-filled leadership, interdependence, and active remembrance of what God has done.

Human Vocation and Cultural Mandate

Exodus 17 presents a scenario where human effort is called upon, but ultimate success rests in God's hands. Moses is called to strike the rock (Exod 17:6), and the people are expected to fight against the Amalekites (Exod 17:9), but in both cases, God provides the outcome—water for survival and victory in battle. This reflects the cultural mandate, where humans are called to participate actively in God's work in the world but always in reliance upon his power and provision. This section informs our calling to be agents of renewal by reminding us that our work—whether in cultivating creation, leading others, or serving our communities—must be done in partnership with God's sovereign will. We are called to steward the resources and opportunities he gives us, but the results are ultimately in his hands. This should lead us to humility and prayerful dependence in our vocations.

Application Today: In today's world, whether in our jobs, families, or ministries, we are reminded that our role is one of stewardship, cultivating the gifts and opportunities God provides. We must work faithfully, but we must also trust that God brings the increase (1 Cor 3:6).

Common Grace and Resistance to Evil

The tension between good and evil is evident in this chapter through the attack by the Amalekites. Their unprovoked aggression against Israel (Exod 17:8) represents the forces of evil and opposition to God's people. In response, God's grace operates to preserve and sustain Israel through the victory provided by his power (Exod 17:13). This shows how God's common grace sustains his people in the face of evil, working through human action (Joshua's leadership in battle) and divine intervention (Moses's uplifted hands symbolizing dependence on God). This section challenges us to resist evil by recognizing that, while we are called to fight against injustice and wrongdoing, it is God who ultimately secures the victory. We resist evil not by our own strength but by relying on God's grace and provision. We see this echoed in the New Testament with Paul's teaching in Eph 6:10–18 about putting on the armor of God to stand against the schemes of the devil.

Application Today: In resisting evil today, whether it's personal temptation or societal injustice, we are reminded that our strength comes from God's grace. We are to take action, as Joshua and Moses did, but we must also recognize that all good gifts and outcomes come from God's sustaining grace (Jas 1:17).

God's Grace and Redemptive History

This section demonstrates God's grace in redemptive history by showing his continuous provision for Israel, despite their grumbling and doubt. The provision of water from the rock (Exod 17:6) is a clear act of grace, as it meets the physical needs of the people despite their lack of faith. Similarly, the victory over the Amalekites (Exod 17:13) is an act of divine grace, highlighting that Israel's survival is not due to their strength but to God's intervention. This section points forward to the greater redemptive work of Christ and his relationship with his covenant people. The New Testament echoes the imagery of water from the rock as a symbol of Christ, the rock from whom living water flows (John 4:13–14; 1 Cor 10:4). Just as Israel's survival depended on the water from the rock, our spiritual survival depends on the grace offered through Christ's sacrificial death and resurrection.

Application Today: In applying this to our lives today, we recognize that, just as Israel's physical and spiritual survival depended on God's grace, our own salvation and perseverance are entirely dependent on God's grace. We are called to participate in God's redemptive work in the world, but it is his grace that sustains us and brings about true transformation in our lives and communities.

Questions for Reflection and Discussion

1. How do we see God's provision in our daily struggles, as Israel saw in the provision of water? Where do you need to trust God's provision more fully in your life?

2. In what areas of life or work do you find yourself relying too much on your own strength rather than trusting in God's provision? How can you practice greater dependence on God in these areas?

3. Just as Israel faced the Amalekites, God's people face various forms of evil and injustice. How can we fight against these challenges while trusting in God's grace to sustain us? What does that look like in practical terms today?

4. How has God been faithful in redemptive history, from Exodus to the present day? How does recognizing God's faithfulness to his covenant help us trust him with our own challenges and uncertainties?

Cultural Mandate and Kingdom Work

Exodus 17 illustrates the relationship between human effort and divine providence, especially in the battle against the Amalekites. Moses's actions in raising his staff during the battle (Exod 17:11) point to the role of human participation in God's mission. However, ultimate success is determined by God's intervention, not solely by human work. This demonstrates that the cultural mandate to cultivate and steward creation must be done in reliance on God's power. Our work, whether spiritual, social, or practical, is always a part of God's broader redemptive mission.

Application Today: This section calls us to engage in work with a balance of human responsibility and divine trust. In our vocations and roles in society, we must cultivate, steward, and build while acknowledging that all growth and success come from God's provision. The New Testament parallel can be seen in Col 3:23–24, where Paul encourages believers to work as though working for the Lord.

Social Mandate and Family Life

The story in Exod 17 reflects the importance of communal effort and leadership in God's people. When Moses's arms grew tired, Aaron and Hur supported him (Exod 17:12), illustrating that even a strong leader needs support from others. This emphasizes the biblical principle that families, communities, and civil society institutions are vital for the well-being of God's people. In today's world, the family remains foundational to building godly communities and advancing God's purposes.

Application Today: Just as Aaron and Hur played a crucial role in supporting Moses, families and communities are called to uphold one another in faith and responsibility. This section reminds us that the strength of godly institutions is not in individualism but in mutual support. In today's context, this can apply to strengthening family bonds, church leadership, and community service.

Liberty, Justice, and God's Kingdom

Exodus 17 reveals God's concern for justice and freedom, as he empowers Israel to defend themselves against an unjust attack by the Amalekites. The victory was not due to Israel's military might but God's intervention. This underscores the biblical principle that true liberty and justice are found in submission to God's sovereignty. As we pursue justice today, this chapter encourages us to seek a form of liberty that is rooted in God's righteousness and not in human autonomy.

Application Today: This section calls us to pursue justice and freedom grounded in God's law and righteousness. It warns against overreliance on human strength or systems. In our fight for political and economic liberty today, we must remember that ultimate justice comes from God alone (Isa 30:18), and our pursuit of liberty must reflect the values of his kingdom.

Spiritual Warfare

Exodus 17 addresses the spiritual and moral challenges faced by God's people. The physical battle against the Amalekites is also a spiritual one, and the victory is won not merely through fighting but through Moses's intercession and reliance on God. Moses raising his hands symbolizes dependence on divine power in the face of evil. This story demonstrates that life is a battleground where God calls his people to stand firm in faith and integrity, relying on him for strength in both physical and spiritual challenges.

Application Today: This section equips believers to approach spiritual warfare with the understanding that victory is rooted in God's power, not human effort alone. Just as Moses depended on God's power to prevail, so must we rely on the full armor of God (Eph 6:10–18) to stand firm against evil forces today. The narrative underscores the necessity of prayer, community support, and faith in facing moral and spiritual challenges.

Questions for Reflection and Discussion

1. How does the story of Israel's battle with the Amalekites illustrate the balance between human effort and reliance on God? In what areas of your life—work, family, or calling—are you being invited to trust more deeply in God's power while remaining faithful in action?

2. What do the roles of Moses, Aaron, and Hur teach us about the importance of community and mutual support in the life of faith? How can we become more intentional about encouraging and sustaining one another in times of spiritual or emotional weariness?

3. How do the themes of provision and protection in this chapter help us recognize God's care in our everyday struggles? Where are you tempted to rely on your own strength, and how might you begin to practice greater dependence on God's daily provision?

4. How does this passage deepen our understanding of God's justice and covenant faithfulness, from Israel's deliverance in the wilderness to our present-day challenges? In what ways can we actively resist injustice and evil today while remaining rooted in trust in God's sustaining grace?

Exodus 18

Context and Analysis

Exodus 18 presents a significant event in Israel's history, where Moses's father-in-law, Jethro, comes to visit and observes Moses's leadership over the people. The historical context is that Israel is newly freed from Egypt and struggling to adjust to life as a liberated nation. Moses is overwhelmed by the task of governing the people and resolving their disputes (Exod 18:13-16). Jethro, an outsider with wisdom, suggests a system of delegation, advising Moses to appoint capable men to help in the administration of justice (Exod 18:17-23). The passage highlights themes of leadership, power dynamics, and divine intervention in guiding leadership structures. Repeated words like "judge" and "burden" emphasize the weight of leadership and the need for a system of shared responsibility. Jethro's advice becomes an example of God using wisdom from outside Israel to shape his people's governance. The divine intervention is subtle but clear in the providential timing of Jethro's visit and his wise counsel.

Spiritual Insights: Basic Anxiety

Moses experiences anxiety in this passage due to the overwhelming responsibility of leading and judging the people (Exod 18:13-16). He is trying to bear the burden of leadership alone, which leaves him exhausted and unable to meet the needs of the people effectively. His fear of not fulfilling his calling properly could be the root of his anxiety. In this situation, Jethro's advice provides spiritual relief by encouraging Moses to trust others and delegate responsibilities (Exod 18:22). Jethro's solution addresses Moses's anxiety by reminding him that God's plan does not require him to carry the burden alone. His response to Moses's anxiety reflects spiritual wisdom—reliance on God through community and shared leadership. Jethro essentially invites Moses to trust others and God more, showing how self-reliance can be harmful.

Problems and Dilemmas

The moral dilemma in this passage revolves around Moses's struggle between his idealized role as the sole leader and the realistic needs of the people. He faces the challenge of whether to continue trying to manage everything alone or to humble himself and accept help from others (Exod 18:17-18). His initial response reflects a sense of duty, but it becomes clear that his method is not sustainable. This dilemma connects with themes of control and faith—Moses must learn to relinquish control and trust that God has provided capable men to assist him. The deeper conflict in this passage is one of leadership: How can a leader remain faithful to their calling while avoiding the temptation of perfectionism and self-reliance?

Themes and Obligations

This passage speaks to God's protection of human leaders by showing how he provides wisdom through others. Moses, though a great prophet, is still vulnerable to the limitations of his humanity. The appointment of other leaders (Exod 18:21-22) shows that God's provision includes the structure of leadership within the community. The moral responsibility placed on Moses—and all leaders—is to recognize their own limitations and to share the burden of leadership. The obligation here is to pursue justice with wisdom and community support, not in isolation. Moses's acceptance of Jethro's advice models humility and a willingness to trust others, which is essential for effective leadership. Leaders today are challenged to think about duty, justice, and character in light of their need for God's guidance and the support of others.

Reflections and Application

In today's context, this passage speaks directly to the modern struggles with burnout, leadership, and control. Just as Moses felt overwhelmed by his responsibilities, many people today feel the weight of trying to meet every expectation in their work, family, or church roles. The concept of the idealized self (the unrealistic expectation of perfection) is clear in Moses's attempt to do everything himself. The lesson from this passage is that delegation, trust, and community are critical to avoiding burnout and embracing God's provision. For leaders, this passage is a reminder that sharing responsibility is not a failure but an act of faith.

God's Sovereignty and Providence

This section reveals God's sovereignty and providence through Jethro's arrival at the right time to provide the wisdom Moses needed. Even though Jethro is not an Israelite, God uses him to guide Moses in restructuring leadership, showing that God's providence often works through unexpected means (Exod 18:17-23). The presence of capable men among the Israelites, able to assist Moses, is also part of God's provision. This passage challenges us to recognize that God's authority is evident not only in miraculous events but also in the wisdom shared through relationships and counsel. Leaders are called to trust God's provision and understand that he orchestrates circumstances to bring about effective leadership and governance.

Covenant Relationship and Faithfulness

This section reflects the covenant relationship between God and his people by showing how God provides for their needs through leadership structures. Moses, as a covenant mediator, is still dependent on God's provision of help through others. The advice Jethro gives aligns with God's covenantal promise to care for his people, even in matters of governance and justice. Faithfulness in this passage is demonstrated by Moses's humility and willingness to implement Jethro's advice. This encourages believers to be faithful not only in leading but also in accepting guidance from others. In the New Testament, this concept is echoed in the way the early church appointed deacons to help with the practical needs of the community (Acts 6:1-7).

Human Vocation and Cultural Mandate

Moses's appointment of leaders to help with the administration of justice aligns with the broader cultural mandate to steward and govern creation effectively. Human vocation in this chapter is illustrated by the responsibility given to capable men who fear God, are trustworthy, and hate dishonest gain (Exod 18:21). This division of labor reflects the call to exercise stewardship not only over creation but also over people and institutions. In today's world, this chapter informs our understanding of work and leadership. It teaches that effective stewardship includes sharing responsibility, trusting others, and structuring leadership in a way that reflects God's order.

Common Grace and Resistance to Evil

The presence of wisdom in Jethro, a non-Israelite, illustrates the concept of common grace. God's grace operates even outside the covenant community to provide wisdom and support to his people. Jethro's advice helps Moses avoid the potential evil of burnout and ineffective leadership, which could harm the entire community.

This section challenges us to resist evil by recognizing that God's grace is at work in the wisdom we receive from others. Whether through believers or nonbelievers, God can provide the insight needed to resist the pressures and evils of overwork and isolation.

God's Grace and Redemptive History

Exodus 18 demonstrates God's grace in redemptive history by showing how he sustains his people through wise leadership. God's provision of capable men to help Moses reflects his ongoing care for Israel as part of his covenant plan. This grace points forward to the New Testament, where Christ, the ultimate leader, appoints his apostles and disciples to carry out his mission (Matt 28:19–20).

The delegation of leadership in this passage serves as a model for the church today, where elders, pastors, and deacons work together to fulfill God's redemptive purposes.

Questions for Reflection and Discussion

1. How does Jethro's advice to Moses about delegation challenge your current approach to leadership or responsibilities in work, family, or ministry?

2. In what ways can we better support leaders in our community or church to prevent burnout and encourage shared leadership?

3. How does the concept of common grace in Jethro's wisdom affect your view of receiving advice or help from those outside the church?

4. How can the principles of stewardship and delegation in Exod 18 shape our understanding of work, leadership, and responsibility in today's world?

Exodus 19

Context and Analysis

The historical context of Exod 19 is the preparation for the giving of the law at Mount Sinai. Israel, having been delivered from Egypt, is now being formed into a covenant nation under God. This passage occurs after the Israelites have experienced God's saving power, but now they must come to understand their responsibilities within God's covenant. The mention of a "kingdom of priests and a holy nation" (Exod 19:6) signals Israel's unique role. The people's fear and awe before God's presence, described with thunder, lightning, and smoke, underscores divine sovereignty and holiness. The repeated phrases about God's descent and the people staying at a distance (Exod 19:12, 21) point to the central themes of divine holiness, control, and mediation between God and man.

Spiritual Insights: Basic Anxiety

The Israelites' fear and awe are palpable as they approach Mount Sinai. The display of God's power through natural phenomena induces fear, reflecting their anxiety about approaching a holy God (Exod 19:16). Their feeling of unworthiness and vulnerability in front of such majesty likely stems from their understanding of God's transcendence. Moses functions as their mediator, indicating that their anxiety is somewhat alleviated when trust is placed in the divinely appointed mediator, instead of themselves. This points to a spiritual reality: anxiety stems from placing trust in self rather than in God's provision, a truth mirrored in Christ's mediation between God and humanity (Heb 4:14–16).

Problems and Dilemmas

The central dilemma in this passage is Israel's preparedness to meet God's holiness. They are called to consecrate themselves (Exod 19:10), emphasizing the tension between their sinful nature and God's demand for holiness. This points to the larger theological issue of how imperfect people can approach a perfect God. The deeper struggle lies in whether Israel can fulfill its calling as a "kingdom of priests" (Exod 19:6). The expectation of being God's treasured possession demands obedience, which reveals a tension between human frailty and divine expectation. In the New Testament, this dilemma is resolved through Christ, who fulfills the law on behalf of God's people (Rom 8:3–4).

Themes and Obligations

The theme of divine protection versus human vulnerability is prevalent in this passage. The Israelites are required to set limits around the mountain because approaching God carelessly could lead to death (Exod 19:12). This underscores the human responsibility to approach God with reverence and in accordance with his commands. The ethical obligations for the original audience include obedience to God's law and acknowledgment of his holiness. Trust in divine provision, seen in Moses's role as mediator, is contrasted with human reliance on self, which would result in danger and death. The call for obedience to God's commands continues to challenge readers today to live in accordance with God's revealed will.

Reflections and Application

This passage speaks directly to modern struggles with anxiety, fear of failure, and reverence for God's holiness. Many today experience feelings of inadequacy in their faith, akin to the Israelites' fear of approaching God. The unrealistic drive for perfection, the idealized self, mirrors Israel's struggle to become a "holy nation." Just as God provided Moses as a mediator, we are reminded that Christ is our perfect mediator who brings us into the presence of God without fear (1 Tim 2:5). The passage also challenges leaders to approach leadership with humility, acknowledging their dependence on God.

God's Sovereignty and Providence

God's sovereignty is displayed in his revelation to Israel and his commands for how they must approach him. He calls the Israelites to be his people, demonstrating that his will governs not only their salvation but also their sanctification. The theophany at Mount Sinai emphasizes that God is above creation and not bound by human constraints (Exod 19:18–19). This should encourage us to trust in God's absolute sovereignty over all things, both in personal life and in societal governance. God is the ultimate authority, and his law provides the foundation for personal and societal order (Rom 13:1–2).

Covenant Relationship and Faithfulness

Exodus 19 marks the formal establishment of God's covenant with Israel, a pivotal moment in redemptive history. From a Dutch Reformed and covenantal perspective, this is not merely a bilateral agreement but the gracious unfolding of God's sovereign initiative to bind himself to a people for his own glory. God reminds Israel of his covenantal faithfulness—how he bore them on eagles' wings and brought them to himself (Exod 19:4). In verse 8, the people enthusiastically agree to obey, yet they do so without full awareness of the weight and cost of covenantal obedience. They are drawn into the mystery of communion with a holy God, not yet grasping the depth of their dependence upon his mercy and mediation. God's designation of Israel as a "kingdom of priests and a holy nation" (Exod 19:6) reflects their calling within the broader covenantal framework: to be a visible community through whom God would bless the nations. This priestly vocation finds its fulfillment in Christ, the true mediator of the new covenant, and extends to the church today. As Peter affirms (1 Pet 2:9), believers are now that royal priesthood, summoned to live faithfully within God's covenant and to display his excellencies to a watching world.

Human Vocation and Cultural Mandate

The vocation of Israel as a "kingdom of priests" and a "holy nation" (Exod 19:6) ties into the cultural mandate. Israel was to be a beacon of holiness, mediating God's grace to the surrounding nations. This reflects the broader calling of humanity to steward and cultivate the world under God's kingship. Christians today share in this mandate, as Christ's disciples are called to participate in God's redemptive mission, working for renewal in every aspect of life, both in labor and rest (Col 3:23).

Common Grace and Resistance to Evil

God's grace operates even in the midst of human imperfection. Israel's inability to approach God without a mediator points to the common grace of having leaders, structures, and laws that maintain societal order and righteousness. By consecrating themselves (Exod 19:10), Israel symbolically resists evil and prepares to meet God. In a similar way, believers today resist evil through obedience and holiness, recognizing that God's grace sustains them even in their imperfection (Jas 4:7).

God's Grace and Redemptive History

This section is a pivotal moment in redemptive history as God formally establishes his covenant with Israel. This covenant anticipates the fuller expression of God's grace in the new covenant, where Christ becomes the ultimate mediator and high priest. God's revelation at Mount Sinai foreshadows the coming of Christ, who fulfills the law and brings reconciliation between God and man (Heb 12:18–24). The grace demonstrated here transforms how we live within the church and the world, encouraging active participation in God's mission to redeem and restore all creation (2 Cor 5:18–20).

Questions for Reflection and Discussion

1. How do the Israelites' fear and awe before God at Mount Sinai reflect our own approach to God's holiness? How should we balance reverence for God with confidence in Christ's mediation?

2. What are some modern-day examples of the "kingdom of priests" concept in which we, as believers, mediate God's grace to others? How can we better live out this calling?

3. In what ways do we struggle with trusting in ourselves rather than in God's provision and sovereignty, as the Israelites did? How does Christ as our mediator help us overcome these struggles?

4. How can we as Christians engage in both cultural renewal and spiritual warfare in our everyday lives, reflecting God's holiness and justice to the world around us?

Cultural Mandate and Kingdom Work

Exodus 19:1–6 highlights the cultural mandate by establishing Israel as a "kingdom of priests" and a "holy nation" (Exod 19:6). This signifies their calling to be stewards of God's covenant and mediators of his grace to the nations. Israel is tasked with displaying God's glory through their obedience and righteous conduct. This stewardship can be applied to our work today by recognizing that all human labor—whether manual, intellectual, or spiritual—is a form of cultivating creation under God's authority. Christians, like Israel, are called to participate in God's mission of renewing the world, including stewardship of natural resources, building healthy communities, and restoring broken systems (Gen 1:28). This is reaffirmed in the New Testament where believers are called to be "a royal priesthood" (1 Pet 2:9), engaging in both work and rest as agents of renewal, trusting in Christ's redemptive work.

Social Mandate and Family Life

The social mandate in Exod 19 revolves around God's establishment of a covenant with his people and the shaping of their communal and family life. God instructs Moses to prepare the people by consecrating themselves for a sacred meeting (Exod 19:10), emphasizing the importance of purity, order, and holiness. The foundation of family and community life is tied to their obedience to God's commands and their collective identity as his chosen people. This section underscores the role of families and communities in nurturing covenant faithfulness. Healthy families and communities are the building blocks of a society that upholds God's order. In today's world, Christians are called to promote godly family life, support civil society institutions like churches and schools, and build communities grounded in biblical values (Eph 6:1–4).

Liberty, Justice, and God's Kingdom

Exodus 19 shows that God's law is central to political and economic liberty. God's covenant with Israel not only sets them apart but also lays down the foundation for justice in their society. The chapter demonstrates that true liberty is found in obedience to God's commands. As God speaks to Moses, he sets clear boundaries (Exod 19:12), showing that liberty within God's kingdom involves submission to his righteous rule. In modern society, pursuing justice involves acknowledging that all freedom and rights are derived from God's law, not from human-made institutions. God's people are encouraged to uphold justice and freedom in a way that mirrors the coming kingdom, advocating for liberty grounded in righteousness and biblical principles (Luke 4:18–19).

Spiritual Warfare

This section reveals the seriousness of approaching God with reverence and the moral challenges Israel faces in maintaining their covenant relationship with God. The warning to not approach the mountain (Exod 19:12–13) reflects the need for spiritual vigilance and integrity. The Israelites are instructed to consecrate themselves, which involves both moral and physical purity (Exod 19:10). This call to holiness points to the ongoing battle against sin, temptation, and spiritual forces of evil that constantly threaten to defile God's people. In the New Testament, Paul reminds believers of the need to put on the armor of God to stand firm in spiritual warfare (Eph 6:10–18). Today, Christians are called to maintain moral integrity by living in obedience to God's word, resisting the pressures of secular culture, and trusting in Christ's victory over sin and evil.

Questions for Reflection and Discussion

1. How does God's dramatic display of holiness at Mount Sinai challenge our view of what it means to approach God with reverence today? What practices can help us cultivate both awe before God's holiness and trust in his grace through Christ?

2. God calls Israel to be a "kingdom of priests and a holy nation." What does this calling look like for believers today, and how can we live out this identity in our homes, churches, and workplaces?

3. The people were commanded to consecrate themselves and maintain physical and moral boundaries before meeting with God. How does this shape our understanding of spiritual preparation, and in what ways are we being called to consecrate ourselves in our present context?

4. In what areas of life do we experience anxiety or a sense of inadequacy when standing before God's expectations? How does Christ as our mediator help us move from fear to faithful obedience in those moments of spiritual tension?

Exodus 20:1-11

Context and Analysis

The historical context of Exod 20:1-11 centers on the giving of the Ten Commandments at Mount Sinai, where God reveals his law to Israel after their deliverance from Egypt. This passage begins with the commandments that outline the proper relationship between God and humanity, emphasizing the exclusivity of God's worship, the rejection of idolatry, and the importance of keeping the Sabbath. The commands about God's identity as the sole object of worship (Exod 20:3) and the sanctity of the Sabbath (Exod 20:8-11) introduce themes of divine sovereignty and human submission. The repeated emphasis on "The LORD your God" reveals God's authority over Israel. Fear of divine judgment and awe at God's power pervade this encounter, teaching that Israel's obedience should arise out of reverence for God, not merely fear of punishment.

Spiritual Insights: Basic Anxiety

The characters, namely the Israelites, likely experienced anxiety due to the overwhelming presence of God at Mount Sinai. Their helplessness before his holiness and commands reflects a deeper spiritual anxiety about their relationship with God. The commands to avoid idolatry (Exod 20:4) and keep the Sabbath (Exod 20:8) directly address human tendencies to control or manipulate spiritual experiences. The people might be tempted to secure comfort through false gods or material representations, but God commands them to trust in him alone. The Sabbath law also speaks to human anxiety about provision and self-sufficiency, reminding them that rest and trust in God's provision are integral to their relationship with him. The New

Testament echoes this in Matt 6:25-34, where Jesus calls believers not to be anxious about their daily needs, but to trust in God's provision.

Problems and Dilemmas

The moral dilemma in this passage involves the struggle to obey the commandments that demand total allegiance to God. The Israelites face the tension between the real self—frail, tempted to self-reliance and idolatry—and the idealized self, which perfectly follows God's laws. For instance, idolatry (Exod 20:4) reflects the human desire to control and define God on human terms. The Sabbath commandment (Exod 20:8) challenges the tension between work and rest, where many struggle to rest in God, believing their worth and security come only from work. This dilemma reveals the deeper conflict between obedience to God's sovereignty and the human tendency toward self-determination.

Themes and Obligations

This passage addresses the theme of God's protection versus human vulnerability. The first four commandments teach that human well-being flows from total dependence on God. Obedience to these laws reflects trust in divine provision (Exod 20:3-11). The Sabbath commandment particularly highlights reliance on God, emphasizing that even in rest, God sustains his people. By ceasing from labor, the Israelites are reminded of God's ultimate control over creation and their lives. Their duty is to acknowledge God's sovereignty in their worship, rest, and service. The ethical obligation placed on the original audience—and on us today—is to revere God, reject idols (material or ideological), and keep the rhythm of work and rest, trusting in his care and sovereignty.

Reflections and Application

The command to rest on the Sabbath (Exod 20:8-11) addresses modern struggles with insecurity and overwork. In our culture of constant productivity, it is easy to place our identity and worth in our achievements rather than in God's provision. The Sabbath commandment teaches us the importance of resting in God's grace rather than striving for unattainable perfection. It also confronts the idealized self, which seeks control and validation through constant activity. Applying this passage today, Christians can find freedom in Christ's invitation to rest (Matt 11:28–30) and take time to reflect on their dependence on God rather than on their own efforts.

God's Sovereignty and Providence

This passage reveals God's absolute sovereignty over creation and human life. He declares himself the LORD, who brought Israel out of slavery, establishing his rightful authority to command their obedience (Exod 20:2). The Sabbath commandment (Exod 20:8–11) points to God as the Creator and sustainer of the universe. As he rested on the seventh day of creation, he calls his people to imitate that rest, showing their dependence on his provision. This section challenges us to submit to God's will, both in how we worship and in how we order our lives, including balancing work and rest.

Covenant Relationship and Faithfulness

Exodus 20:1–11 reflects the covenant relationship between God and his people. God's law is not merely a set of moral rules but an expression of the covenant, where he claims Israel as his own and requires their exclusive devotion. The faithfulness of God, seen in his deliverance of Israel (Exod 20:2), calls for a faithful response from his people. In today's context, this covenant relationship continues for Christians through Christ, who fulfilled the law on our behalf (Matt 5:17), and we live out this covenant by honoring God through worship and obedience.

Human Vocation and Cultural Mandate

This passage aligns with the cultural mandate by emphasizing that human beings are called to live under God's authority, reflecting his character in their work and rest. The command to keep the Sabbath (Exod 20:8–11) teaches that our labor is not ultimate, but is part of a rhythm that includes rest and worship. Christians today can apply this by understanding their vocations as ways to cultivate and steward creation while honoring God's design for rest and renewal.

Common Grace and Resistance to Evil

The prohibition against idolatry (Exod 20:4) highlights the battle between good and evil, where human hearts are constantly tempted to turn away from God and toward false gods. God's grace is seen in the provision of his law, which guides his people away from destructive practices. This section challenges believers to resist the pull of idolatry in any form, whether materialism, success, or other worldly temptations, and to recognize that all good gifts come from God (Jas 1:17).

God's Grace and Redemptive History

God's grace is evident in the fact that he gives the law as part of his redemptive plan for Israel, following their deliverance from Egypt. The law, especially the Sabbath command, points forward to the rest and redemption that are fully realized in Christ (Heb 4:9–10). In this chapter, the giving of the law demonstrates God's desire to guide his people in righteousness and holiness, leading them toward the ultimate redemption that will come through the work of Jesus.

Questions for Reflection and Discussion

1. How does the command to keep the Sabbath challenge our modern understanding of work, rest, and identity?

2. In what ways do we see idolatry (whether material or ideological) present in our culture, and how can we resist its influence in our own lives?

3. How does the commandment to worship God alone help us navigate today's cultural pressures to prioritize other things above our relationship with him?

4. What does it look like to live out the covenant relationship with God through faithful obedience in our daily work, worship, and family life? How can we cultivate this relationship in practical ways?

Cultural Mandate and Kingdom Work

In Exod 20:1–11, the cultural mandate is reflected in the call to keep the Sabbath holy (Exod 20:8). This commandment reminds humanity of their responsibility to cultivate and steward creation while balancing work and rest. By establishing a rhythm of six days of work and one day of rest (Exod 20:9–10), God emphasizes the importance of both diligent work and restorative rest. This informs our modern understanding of vocation, reminding us that work is a form of stewardship over creation, and rest is an acknowledgment of God's ultimate sovereignty over all creation. This mirrors the creation pattern in Genesis, where God worked for six days and rested on the seventh (Exod 20:11), setting a divine model for human work and rest. Today, we are called to be agents of renewal, not only through our work but also by participating in God's mission of restoring all things, including our approach to work-life balance. Jesus, in Matt 11:28–30, invites us to find rest in him, which aligns with the Sabbath commandment.

Social Mandate and Family Life

This section highlights the importance of both social order and family life. The Sabbath commandment (Exod 20:8–11) is a social institution that binds the people of God together. It is not only a personal command but one that is to be observed by families, servants, and even animals. The practice of resting on the Sabbath teaches the importance of caring for those under our charge and upholding God's order within the family structure and community. The command to observe the Sabbath serves as a reminder of God's covenant faithfulness and invites families to reorient themselves around God as the center of their lives. The Sabbath becomes a symbol of liberation, as seen in Deut 5:15, where God reminds Israel that they were once slaves in Egypt and are now free to rest. This applies today as families seek to establish rhythms of worship and rest that prioritize God's rule and reflect his order in creation.

Liberty, Justice, and God's Kingdom

This section reflects God's concern for justice and liberty through the concept of the Sabbath, which protects the marginalized and vulnerable. The command to give rest to all within the household, including servants and animals (Exod 20:10), shows God's concern for economic and social justice. The Sabbath provides relief from the constant pressure of labor and serves as a reminder of the freedom God gave Israel from slavery in Egypt (Deut 5:15). Theologically, the Sabbath is a call to trust in God's provision, as the Israelites were called to cease from their work and trust that God would sustain them. This has significant implications for pursuing justice today, especially in a world where economic and social inequalities exist. Observing the Sabbath and trusting in God's provision encourages believers to pursue liberty and justice in ways that reflect the coming kingdom of God, where justice and righteousness will prevail (Isa 9:7).

Spiritual Warfare

The commandments in Exod 20:1–11 address the spiritual and moral challenges faced by God's people. The call to worship God alone (Exod 20:3), avoid idolatry (Exod 20:4), and keep the Sabbath (Exod 20:8) represent key areas of spiritual warfare. The Israelites were surrounded by cultures that worshiped multiple gods, and these commands called them to spiritual integrity. Worshiping the one true God and resting on the Sabbath was a countercultural act that reinforced the need for moral courage in the face of surrounding temptations. Today, these principles apply as we face spiritual and moral battles in a world that often prioritizes materialism, self-reliance, and neglect of worship. The Sabbath commandment also teaches that spiritual rest and moral integrity are deeply intertwined. By honoring the Sabbath, believers are reminded that they are not defined by their productivity or achievements but by their identity in God. Hebrews 4:9–11 reminds us that there remains a Sabbath rest for God's people, urging believers to hold fast to faith and trust in God's provision.

Questions for Reflection and Discussion

1. How does observing the Sabbath in our modern world challenge our understanding of work and rest? In what ways can we actively pursue rest that honors God?

2. How can families incorporate practices of Sabbath rest and worship that reflect God's command to center their lives around him? What challenges do families face today in upholding this command?

3. In what ways does the Sabbath reflect God's concern for justice and economic liberty? How can we apply these principles in our daily lives, particularly in how we treat those under our care or influence?

4. How does keeping the Sabbath equip us to engage in spiritual warfare and maintain moral integrity in a world filled with distractions and temptations?

Exodus 20:12-21

Context and Analysis

The second half of the Decalogue moves from commands about honoring God to instructions for life in covenantal community, exposing a different layer of basic human anxiety—not about God's holiness, but about human frailty, injustice, and disorder. The command to honor one's father and mother (Exod 20:12) addresses our fears about rejection, legacy, and broken authority. The prohibitions against murder, adultery, theft, false witness, and coveting (Exod 20:13-17) confront deeper fears—fear of loss, betrayal, scarcity, and social instability. These commandments call the people to resist fear-based self-preservation and instead embrace a communal life rooted in mutual respect, truth, and contentment. The people's fearful reaction to God's presence (Exod 20:18-19) reflects the weight of these divine demands. Yet Moses reframes their fear—not as terror, but as reverence that leads to obedience (Exod 20:20). This fear, rightly directed, becomes the foundation for trust and moral formation.

Spiritual Insights: Basic Anxiety

As the second half of the Decalogue turns toward human relationships, the inner anxiety of the Israelites shifts from fear of divine transcendence to the challenge of trust in social and relational order. Honoring parents (Exod 20:12) touches on the fear of generational breakdown and loss of belonging. The commandments against murder (Exod 20:13), adultery (Exod 20:14), and theft (Exod 20:15) address human anxieties around security, betrayal, and provision. False witness (Exod 20:16) reveals fear about reputation and social standing, while coveting (Exod 20:17) exposes a deep insecurity of not having enough or being enough. These commands collectively confront the disordered desires driven by fear—fear of loss, fear of vulnerability, fear of being overlooked. The people's trembling response at Sinai (Exod 20:18-19) illustrates this basic anxiety: they beg for distance between themselves and God, needing a mediator. Yet Moses reminds them that reverence and fear of the LORD are meant to keep them from sin, not to paralyze them. The law invites them—and us—to place trust in God's design for human relationships, not in self-protection or comparison.

Problems and Dilemmas

These commandments present moral and spiritual challenges that go beyond mere behavior and reach into the condition of the heart. Honoring one's parents becomes difficult when relationships are broken or when cultural values conflict with biblical ones. The prohibition against murder challenges not only acts of violence but also anger, resentment, and indifference to human dignity. Adultery implicates not only physical acts but also mental infidelity and misuse of desire. The prohibition of theft forces us to examine not only whether we take, but whether we fail to give—whether in wages, time, or generosity. Bearing false witness raises the issue of everyday deceit, gossip, or silence in the face of injustice. Coveting, perhaps the most inward of all, uncovers our tendency to compare, envy, and grasp for what God has not given. The dilemma is clear: we often want the fruits of justice and peace without the moral discipline these commandments require. Israel, like us, faces the tension between what God commands and what the heart desires.

Reflections and Application

These commandments offer clear and urgent guidance for modern believers. Honoring parents can look like advocacy for elder care or repairing estranged relationships. The prohibition of murder calls for a culture of life that includes protecting the vulnerable, addressing violence, and rooting out hatred. Adultery is resisted not only through marital faithfulness but also by cultivating integrity in thoughts, affections, and digital habits. Theft encompasses wage justice, economic transparency, and generous stewardship. Bearing false witness cautions us against gossip, misinformation, and self-serving narratives. The command against coveting might be the most radical in a consumerist society—it challenges us to be deeply content, to resist the idolatry of comparison, and to find our sufficiency in Christ.

Living out these commands invites us into a distinctive life of holiness in every sphere.

God's Sovereignty and Providence

These laws reflect not only God's moral expectations but his providential ordering of human society. God's sovereignty is evident in his right to establish ethical boundaries, and his providence is displayed in the protective nature of these commands. They are designed to promote flourishing and justice in human relationships. The people's fear (Exod 20:18) is not a flaw in the narrative—it is the appropriate response to encountering divine sovereignty. Yet God does not abandon them to their fear; he speaks through Moses, offering clarity and assurance. His commands reveal his care, showing that divine law is not a burden but a provision for life.

Covenant Relationship and Faithfulness

These commands are covenantal at their core. They are given to a people who have been delivered by grace and are now called to walk in faithful response. Obedience is not transactional—it is relational. It expresses loyalty to the God who saves. These commandments outline how the redeemed are to live with one another, making visible the invisible realities of the covenant. In a world of fractured relationships, living according to this moral pattern becomes a testimony of God's faithfulness and a witness to his redemptive power.

Human Vocation and Cultural Mandate

The implications of these commands reach every corner of human vocation. Families, workplaces, governments, schools, and neighborhoods all thrive when built on the foundations of respect, truthfulness, justice, and contentment. To honor parents is to protect cultural memory and wisdom. To preserve life and marriage is to promote societal health. To act justly with property and speech is to uphold dignity and truth. To resist coveting is to steward desires in a world bent on excess. Living vocationally within the framework of these laws reflects God's purposes in creation: order, fruitfulness, and community.

Common Grace and Resistance to Evil

These laws operate not only within the church but within wider society, forming the basis of a just and ordered life through God's common grace. Even in nonbelieving cultures, echoes of these commandments are found in laws against murder, theft, and perjury. These laws preserve life and prevent chaos. Yet for believers, they also serve as a form of resistance—resistance to the dehumanizing forces of violence, greed, lust, and envy that tear communities apart. When the people stood at a distance and asked for a mediator (Exod 20:19), they acknowledged their need for help to live in such righteousness. Today, we resist evil not only through outward compliance, but by the inward transformation enabled by Christ and the Spirit.

God's Grace and Redemptive History

The final verses of this passage show the people standing in fear, but God speaking through Moses to assure them. This image of fear and mediation points ahead to the redemptive work of Christ. The commandments highlight the depth of human sin—internal and external—and the necessity of grace. Jesus not only affirms these commands but deepens their meaning, showing their heart-level intent (Matt 5:21–48). Through his perfect obedience, he fulfills the law and gives his righteousness to those who trust in him. Now, believers do not relate to the law as a crushing weight, but as a guide in sanctification. The law is a mirror that shows our need for Christ, a map for grateful obedience, and a means by which God shapes his people to reflect his holiness and love.

Liberty, Justice, and God's Kingdom

God's concern for justice and liberty is evident in this passage, particularly in the commandments forbidding murder, adultery, theft, and bearing false witness (Exod 20:13–16). These laws aim to protect personal rights and the sanctity of relationships, ensuring that individuals are free from harm, exploitation, and deceit. The prohibition against coveting (Exod 20:17) addresses the heart's desire for material possessions or relationships that belong to others, showing that true justice and liberty start within. From a libertarian perspective, these commandments highlight the need for personal responsibility and the protection of private property and personal integrity, grounded in God's righteousness. Galatians 5:13 teaches that Christian liberty should be used to serve others rather than indulge in selfish desires. These commandments reflect the kingdom of God, where justice and righteousness reign, calling believers to pursue liberty through godly living.

Spiritual Warfare

The commandments in this passage provide a framework for moral integrity, guiding God's people in their spiritual battles. Each of the prohibitions—against murder, adultery, theft, false witness, and coveting—addresses the heart's potential to turn away from God's will. These commandments call the Israelites to live with integrity before God, resisting the temptation to harm others or indulge in selfish desires. This passage serves as a battleground for the soul, where God's people are called to resist evil by following his commandments and cultivating love, honesty, and respect for others. Ephesians 6:11–12 reminds believers that the struggle is not just against flesh and blood but against spiritual forces of evil, emphasizing the need for moral integrity in the Christian walk. Following these commandments strengthens our spiritual armor and enables us to stand firm in a world filled with moral challenges.

Questions for Reflection and Discussion

1. How does honoring one's parents invite us to reflect on God's design for authority and generational faithfulness? In what ways can this commandment be honored even when family relationships are strained or imperfect?

2. What are the practical implications of the commandments against murder, adultery, and theft in a culture that normalizes violence, sexual brokenness, and economic exploitation? How might we embody justice and compassion as individuals and communities?

3. How does bearing false witness go beyond lying and speak to how we represent others in our words and actions, both online and in real life? How can we cultivate truth telling in a world of spin, gossip, and misinformation?

4. In a society built on constant comparison and accumulation, how can we practice resistance through the command not to covet? What practices help us grow in gratitude and contentment, especially in our consumer-driven culture?

Exodus 21:1-11

Context and Analysis

Exodus 21:1-11 addresses the laws regarding Hebrew servants, providing guidelines for how they should be treated and the duration of their service. In the historical and cultural context, servitude was common in the ancient Near East, and these laws served to regulate an institution that existed within Israel, but with strict limits to ensure justice and human dignity. These laws reflect a God who cares about the vulnerable and provides for their protection in an imperfect world. Key phrases like "freedom" (Exod 21:2) and "rights" (Exod 21:10) underscore the importance of fairness and justice. The repeated emphasis on care for servants suggests themes of protection, responsibility, and God's intervention in human systems of power to ensure fairness and compassion. Unlike other ancient cultures where servitude could be brutal and lifelong, Israel was called to remember their own deliverance from Egypt and treat others with kindness.

Spiritual Insights: Basic Anxiety

The law concerning Hebrew servants in this passage highlights anxieties related to vulnerability, power, and control. Both the servant and master may experience insecurity: the servant is vulnerable to mistreatment, and the master is concerned with obedience and productivity. A servant might feel helpless, especially when facing extended servitude, but the passage stresses that the servant is to be set free in the seventh year (Exod 21:2), reflecting God's concern for justice and rest. This divine limitation on servitude encourages trust in God rather than self-expansion or dominance. Anxiety can arise when people forget God's ultimate provision and sovereignty. The passage encourages the Israelites to trust in God's law and plan for justice, promoting a relationship based on God's provision rather than exploitation. Matthew 6:25-34 reminds us not to worry, for God provides for our needs.

Problems and Dilemmas

This passage raises moral dilemmas about how power and authority should be exercised, particularly regarding servitude and economic justice. The dilemma for the master is whether to treat the servant according to the spirit of God's law—with kindness and fairness—or to exploit them for economic gain. The servant, on the other hand, faces the dilemma of choosing between freedom after six years or remaining in service under good conditions (Exod 21:5-6). This underscores a deeper tension between freedom and obligation, or between the real self—bound in servitude—and the idealized self—seeking autonomy or divine favor. The text invites reflection on how authority can either be abused or used to reflect God's justice. The passage challenges readers to ask whether their leadership or use of power reflects God's values of justice and mercy, or selfish interests.

Themes and Obligations

The primary theme of Exod 21:1-11 is God's protection of the vulnerable and the limits placed on human authority. The master's power is not absolute; it is governed by God's laws that ensure servants are treated fairly and given their freedom in the seventh year (Exod 21:2). The obligation on the master is to act justly and responsibly, recognizing the servant's human dignity. This text challenges readers to think about their duty toward the vulnerable in their own context. In what ways do we use power or authority in our homes, workplaces, or communities? How do we treat those who are under our care or authority? This passage calls us to use authority with compassion, reflecting God's own mercy. James 2:13 reminds us that mercy triumphs over judgment.

Reflections and Application

Exodus 21:1-11 can speak to modern struggles with insecurity and fear of economic or social vulnerability. While the context of servitude may not directly apply to today's world, the principles of justice, compassion, and fair treatment of others remain relevant. The laws here highlight the tension between power and compassion—reminding us that we are all stewards of the roles and authority we hold. The passage challenges modern readers to reflect on how we treat those in dependent or vulnerable positions (e.g., employees, marginalized individuals) and how we can promote fairness and justice in personal and societal relationships. Colossians 4:1 exhorts masters (or those in positions of authority) to treat their servants (or subordinates) with justice and fairness, knowing that they, too, have a Master in heaven.

God's Sovereignty and Providence

This section reveals God's sovereignty in shaping the moral and legal frameworks that govern society. The laws concerning servants are not arbitrary but reflect God's providential care for his people, even in economic systems and relationships of power. By setting a limit on the duration of servitude, God demonstrates his concern for justice, rest, and renewal. His providence ensures that servants are not permanently oppressed but have the opportunity for freedom, a reflection of Israel's own deliverance from Egypt. This challenges believers to recognize God's authority in all areas of life, including economic and social systems, and to trust in his sovereign plan for justice. Proverbs 29:7 emphasizes that the righteous care about justice for the poor, which aligns with God's providence and moral vision.

Covenant Relationship and Faithfulness

Exodus 21:1–11 reflects the covenant relationship between God and Israel, where God's people are called to live according to his laws of justice and mercy. These laws regarding servitude are a reminder of the Israelites' own liberation from slavery in Egypt, and thus their treatment of servants reflects their covenant faithfulness to God. The passage underscores that faithfulness to the covenant involves not only worship and rituals but also ethical treatment of others, particularly the vulnerable. In today's world, living out covenant obligations includes being faithful stewards of justice in our relationships and workplaces. This passage encourages believers to reflect God's faithfulness in their own lives by acting justly and compassionately. Micah 6:8 reminds us that God requires us to act justly, love mercy, and walk humbly with him.

Human Vocation and Cultural Mandate

This passage reflects the human vocation to steward relationships and resources with justice and care. While servitude may not be directly applicable today, the principles of fair treatment, economic justice, and concern for the vulnerable remain central to our cultural mandate to cultivate and develop society in a way that reflects God's righteousness. The laws governing servitude remind us that God cares about how we engage in work, relationships, and social structures. Believers are called to steward authority, wealth, and resources with fairness and responsibility, promoting justice and human dignity. Ephesians 6:5–9 calls for mutual respect between masters and servants, with a recognition that we are all ultimately serving God.

Common Grace and Resistance to Evil

Exodus 21:1–11 portrays the tension between human power and God's grace. The laws governing servitude show how God's grace operates even in imperfect systems, providing boundaries to prevent abuse and oppression. These laws act as a form of common grace, limiting the potential for evil within a fallen world by regulating how people are treated. They remind us that even in flawed systems, God's grace is at work to sustain justice and mercy. This passage challenges believers to resist evil in whatever form it may take—whether through exploitation or unfair treatment of others—and to act as agents of God's grace in a world that often ignores his commands. Romans 12:21 calls us to overcome evil with good, reflecting this principle.

God's Grace and Redemptive History

This passage demonstrates God's grace in redemptive history by pointing to the ultimate liberation that God offers his people. Just as the laws governing servitude provided a path to freedom in the seventh year, they foreshadow God's greater redemptive work in Christ, who liberates us from the bondage of sin. The passage reminds us that God's justice and mercy are intertwined, and that his law points us toward his redemptive plan for humanity. In the New Testament, Jesus proclaims that he came to set the captives free (Luke 4:18), fulfilling the deeper spiritual freedom that the law in Exodus anticipates. This section transforms how we live by reminding us of the redemptive work of God in every area of life—whether in justice, relationships, or economic systems.

Cultural Mandate and Kingdom Work

The cultural mandate given to humanity in Genesis to cultivate, steward, and develop creation is reflected in Exod 21:1-11 in the laws regulating the treatment of servants. These laws suggest that even in relationships of servitude, there is a call to justice, care, and renewal. The master's responsibility to release a servant after six years (Exod 21:2) aligns with the biblical rhythm of work and rest, showing how God provides for renewal and restoration. This also reflects the broader kingdom principle that God's people are to cultivate relationships of dignity and care, mirroring God's justice in all human interactions. The call to be agents of renewal means that believers today should seek to implement fairness and justice in work environments, recognizing the image of God in every person (Gen 1:27) and ensuring that systems of labor reflect God's righteousness and compassion.

Social Mandate and Family Life

This section also touches upon the family dynamics of God's people. The provision for servants, including their ability to remain in service if they choose to stay with their family (Exod 21:5-6), highlights the importance of preserving family unity. The text reinforces the importance of familial and social structures that promote well-being, loyalty, and care. By allowing a servant to choose to stay with their master to be with their family, the passage emphasizes the value of relationships and community ties. In today's context, this teaches us to uphold the sanctity of family, recognizing that strong, godly families are vital for advancing God's purposes. Families, as foundational social institutions, should be places where justice, compassion, and biblical values are practiced (Eph 6:1-4).

Liberty, Justice, and God's Kingdom

Exodus 21:1-11 reflects God's concern for justice and liberty by mandating the release of servants after six years (Exod 21:2). This law provides a balance between work and freedom, showing that servitude in Israel was never meant to be permanent or oppressive, as it was in other ancient cultures. It affirms the principle that God's justice liberates and restores, reflecting the broader redemptive narrative where God liberates his people from oppression (e.g., Israel's exodus from Egypt). This passage challenges us to pursue liberty and justice in ways that reflect God's kingdom values. Believers are called to promote freedom from exploitation and to advocate for systems where economic and political liberty are grounded in righteousness. Galatians 5:1 reminds us that Christ has set us free for the sake of freedom, not to fall back into bondage of any kind, whether physical or spiritual.

Spiritual Warfare

Exodus 21:1–11 also has implications for spiritual warfare and moral integrity. The way masters were commanded to treat servants with fairness and dignity reflects God's demand for moral integrity in every sphere of life. The law forbids exploitative treatment, and the option for a servant to voluntarily remain out of love for their master (Exod 21:5–6) demonstrates a relationship built on trust, loyalty, and integrity rather than domination. The spiritual challenge for God's people is to live in a way that reflects God's character in all interactions, particularly in positions of power or authority. This text calls believers to stand firm against exploitation and to act in moral uprightness, knowing that God's kingdom is advanced through justice and righteousness. Ephesians 6:12 reminds us that we are in a spiritual battle, and integrity in our dealings with others is part of our testimony in that battle.

Questions for Reflection and Discussion

1. How does the command to release Hebrew servants after six years reflect God's vision for justice, mercy, and human dignity? In what ways can this principle inform our approach to labor, long-term commitments, and equitable treatment in the workplace or broader society today?

2. What does this passage teach us about the responsible use of authority and power, particularly in relationships where one party may be more vulnerable than the other? How can we ensure our leadership—whether at home, in church, or at work—reflects the character of God, who values compassion, justice, and protection of the weak?

3. How does the structure of these laws reflect a balance between personal freedom and communal responsibility? How should Christians today navigate situations where obligations, such as in family or professional roles, seem to limit personal freedom?

4. In what ways does this passage demonstrate the function of God's law as a form of common grace, restraining injustice and protecting

human worth? How can we embody these values practically by advocating for justice, fair treatment, and care for the marginalized in our communities today?

Exodus 21:12-36

Context and Analysis

This passage is part of the legal code given to Israel, specifically addressing issues of personal injury and liability. The historical and cultural background is rooted in a society where the principles of justice, compensation, and proportionality ("an eye for an eye") were foundational for maintaining social order. In the context of the ancient Near East, laws such as these were necessary to promote justice and prevent escalating cycles of violence. The key characters in these legal situations respond to power and vulnerability by seeking justice through compensation and reparation, not revenge. Repeated phrases like "must be put to death" (Exod 21:12, 15, 16) emphasize the seriousness of offenses involving human life, while the principle of proportional justice—seen in verses like "an eye for an eye" (Exod 21:24)—suggests God's concern for fairness and preventing excess punishment in the presence of God (Lev 24:20). This theme of control and divine justice reveals a God who values life and equity, contrasting with the common practices of retribution in surrounding cultures.

Spiritual Insights: Basic Anxiety

The legal cases presented in this passage reflect various fears and anxieties about violence, injury, and justice. For those involved, the source of fear is rooted in either the oppression of violent acts or the potential lack of justice. The different responses to these anxieties are governed by God's law, which provides a framework for handling disputes. For instance, the person guilty of manslaughter could flee to a city of refuge, reflecting a trust in divine provision for mercy (Exod 21:13). Others, like the master whose ox kills a person (Exod 21:28-29), are held accountable and face the consequences of negligence. Anxiety is mitigated when individuals place trust in God's legal and moral system rather than seeking to resolve issues through vengeance or self-reliance. By trusting in God's commands, the people could find peace and order within the community.

Problems and Dilemmas

The passage presents moral and spiritual dilemmas such as how to handle involuntary manslaughter (Exod 21:13) and the fair compensation for bodily harm (Exod 21:18-19). These dilemmas connect to themes of fear, control, and faith. How does one maintain justice while ensuring compassion and mercy? The passage highlights the tension between the real self (an individual in a sinful world prone to violence and injury) and the ideal self (one who upholds justice and righteousness as God's law requires). There are deeper conflicts related to obedience and leadership, especially when those in positions of authority (e.g., masters) are held to strict standards of responsibility. The laws concerning oxen (Exod 21:28-32) show how negligence or carelessness can lead to legal and moral responsibility, raising questions about leadership and stewardship of resources and animals.

Themes and Obligations

Exodus 21:12-36 addresses the theme of God's protection versus human vulnerability. God's laws are given to protect the vulnerable, ensuring that justice is served when life is threatened. The text places moral and ethical responsibilities on the people to uphold these laws, to respect life, and to maintain fairness in all dealings. This passage challenges readers to think about duty and justice, especially regarding the protection of life and the consequences of one's actions. The characters in this passage pursue noble goals—ensuring justice and protection—but they are also hindered by self-interest and negligence at times. For instance, the owner of a dangerous animal is held accountable for their failure to restrain it, demonstrating the ethical responsibility to protect others from harm (Exod 21:29-30).

Reflections and Application

This passage speaks to modern struggles with insecurity, fear of failure, and anxiety about justice. We live in a world where violence, accidents, and harm are real possibilities, and there are deep concerns about whether justice will be served in every situation. The concept of the idealized self may come into play when individuals feel the unrealistic pressure to achieve perfect justice in every situation. In a broken world, we must recognize our limitations and turn to God's law for guidance on what is just and fair. For modern readers, this passage encourages a balanced approach to justice that upholds the value of life and responsibility without devolving into retribution or lawlessness. In today's world, these laws speak to contexts of leadership, community challenges, and personal struggles with accountability and justice.

God's Sovereignty and Providence

This section reveals God's sovereignty and providence by establishing a system of justice that reflects his character. God's laws are not arbitrary but are rooted in his holiness and desire for righteousness among his people. The laws also acknowledge human sinfulness and imperfection, providing ways to handle situations where accidents or negligence lead to harm. The overarching message is that God governs all aspects of life, including legal and ethical matters, and his providence extends even to seemingly mundane issues like personal injury or property disputes. Trusting in God's sovereignty means recognizing that his laws are meant to reflect his order and justice in society. Romans 13:1–2 emphasizes that all authority is from God and that we are to submit to his ordained structures for justice and order.

Covenant Relationship and Faithfulness

This section reflects the covenant relationship between God and his people through the legal code given to protect life and promote justice. These laws are part of the covenant God established with Israel at Sinai, showing how his people are to live in a way that reflects his holiness and justice. Living out the covenant obligations in today's world means upholding justice, protecting the vulnerable, and acting responsibly in all areas of life. The faithfulness of God in giving such detailed laws shows his care for every aspect of human life. This should encourage us to be faithful in our responsibilities to God, the church, and the broader community, ensuring that justice is served in our dealings with others. The New Testament echoes this covenantal obligation in passages like Matt 22:37–39, where Jesus emphasizes love for God and neighbor as the fulfillment of the law.

Human Vocation and Cultural Mandate

The responsibilities given to God's people in this chapter align with the call to exercise stewardship and care over creation. The laws regarding personal injury, property, and responsibility show that God's people are to manage their lives, property, and relationships in a way that promotes justice and harmony. This aligns with the broader cultural mandate from Gen 1:28 to cultivate and steward the world responsibly. The call to work and serve as part of God's kingdom involves ensuring that justice prevails in our communities, workplaces, and societal structures. These laws remind us that part of our vocation is to reflect God's justice in the way we live and interact with others.

Common Grace and Resistance to Evil

This section portrays the tension between good and evil through its regulations that prevent violence and exploitation. God's grace operates even in the midst of evil by providing a just system of laws that restrain sinful behavior and protect the innocent. The regulations about manslaughter and bodily harm demonstrate how God's grace operates in ensuring that justice is done and that evil is resisted. The restraint of evil through God's laws is an act of common grace that upholds society. Believers are called to resist evil while recognizing that all good gifts, including justice and order, come from God. This passage calls for wisdom in resisting the temptation to take matters into one's own hands but instead to trust in God's established systems of justice (Rom 12:19).

God's Grace and Redemptive History

This section demonstrates God's grace in redemptive history by showing that even in legal matters, God is concerned with justice and fairness. The laws given in this passage are not merely regulations but part of God's redemptive plan to establish a just and holy people. These laws reflect the moral order that God desires for his people, pointing toward the ultimate justice and grace found in Christ. The New Testament reflects this redemptive grace in passages like Rom 5:8, where God's love and justice meet in the sacrifice of Jesus. God's grace in this chapter transforms how we live, both within the church and in the world, by calling us to uphold justice, protect life, and act responsibly in all areas of life.

Social Mandate and Family Life

This section highlights social order through laws that protect individuals from harm, including issues of family and community responsibility. For example, verses 15-17 discuss the severe consequences for dishonoring parents or harming family members, emphasizing the importance of family dynamics in God's social order. In today's context, this reminds us of the social mandate to uphold family integrity and respect for authority within households (Eph 6:1-3). A strong family structure is critical for advancing God's purposes because it nurtures justice, obedience, and mutual care, providing stability for communities. By applying these principles, we build societies that reflect God's order.

Liberty, Justice, and God's Kingdom

Exodus 21:12-36 reveals God's concern for justice and liberty, particularly through laws regarding manslaughter, negligence, and property damage. Justice is served through restitution, proportionality ("an eye for an eye" in verse 24), and the protection of life. These laws align with God's righteousness and call for fairness in legal matters, promoting both political and economic liberty. In our modern context, this calls for a justice system that respects individual rights and freedoms while maintaining social responsibility. God's kingdom is characterized by justice, and as we pursue liberty in areas like economic freedom or legal fairness, we do so in alignment with the coming kingdom of God, reflecting his values in our societies (Isa 61:8; Luke 4:18-19).

Spiritual Warfare

This passage touches on the moral integrity required to live righteously in a community. Laws governing manslaughter, personal injury, and negligence reveal the spiritual challenge of managing human relationships justly. For example, when a person is responsible for harm caused by an animal (Exod 21:28-36), it emphasizes the moral responsibility we carry for the welfare of others. In terms of spiritual warfare, living with integrity by obeying God's laws is part of resisting sin and injustice in the world. It equips us to stand firm in situations where moral challenges arise, knowing that God's justice and righteousness must govern our behavior. Ephesians 6:12-14 reminds us to stand firm with righteousness as a defense against the spiritual forces of evil, and Exod 21 provides practical guidance on living justly in community.

Questions for Reflection and Discussion

1. What do the laws in this passage teach us about the value of human life and justice in God's eyes? How can we apply these principles in today's society?

2. How does the concept of proportional justice ("an eye for an eye") guide us in our understanding of fairness and responsibility today? How can we apply this in conflict resolution within our communities?

3. What are some modern situations where the principles of justice and responsibility in this passage might help us make ethical decisions in leadership, community, or family life?

4. How does this passage reflect God's sovereignty in establishing justice and order? How does recognizing God's authority in legal and ethical matters influence the way we trust and submit to his will today?

Exodus 22:1-15

Context and Analysis

Exodus 22:1–15 is part of the Mosaic law that provides detailed civil laws for the newly freed Israelite society. These laws address the protection of property, dealing with theft, damage to animals and property, and personal responsibility. The background of these laws reflects a nomadic, agrarian society in which livestock and land were central to daily life and economic stability. The passage emphasizes restitution and personal responsibility for wrongdoing. The themes of justice, accountability, and fairness are central. Repeated words and phrases like "restitution" (Exod 22:3) and "make full restitution" (Exod 22:5) emphasize the importance of restoring what was lost, highlighting God's concern for fairness, responsibility, and the proper use of power over others.

Spiritual Insights: Basic Anxiety

In these laws, we see how God addresses the basic anxiety people might have regarding property loss, theft, and damage. Anxiety over possessions, which were crucial for survival, could lead to fear and conflict. The Israelites might have been anxious about their livelihoods and the fear of losing their property. This anxiety is countered by laws that ensure restitution and justice. Coping mechanisms can be identified in the forms of taking responsibility (Exod 22:6), making restitution, or denying responsibility (Exod 22:11), depending on the circumstances. This passage encourages the community to trust in God's provision and the social system he ordained, rather than resorting to self-protection or dishonesty. Trusting in God's law ensures the welfare of the community and individual relationships.

Problems and Dilemmas

The passage brings out dilemmas related to justice and restitution. It asks questions like: How should a person be held accountable for damage or loss they cause? Should restitution always be equal to the loss, or should it go beyond that? The real self, a person struggling with guilt or wrongdoing, is challenged by the expectation of full restitution, reflecting the ideal self of integrity and honesty before God. This passage shows the tension between doing what is right (honoring God's law) and human tendencies to protect oneself. For example, in verse 14, if a person borrows an animal and it is injured, they must make restitution, presenting a moral dilemma over personal responsibility and the cost of doing what is right.

Themes and Obligations

Exodus 22:1–15 speaks to the theme of God's protection and the moral obligation to care for others' possessions. The laws show that God values justice and fairness in human relationships, ensuring that those who wrong others are held accountable. The repeated command for restitution underscores the duty of the wrongdoer to restore what was lost or damaged. The text places moral responsibilities on both the victim and the wrongdoer, obligating each to act justly and uphold fairness. This challenges the reader to think about duty, justice, and responsibility in a society. In God's community, integrity, and justice are paramount, and the characters' responses to these laws show that they must either embrace justice or be hindered by self-interest.

Reflections and Application

This passage speaks directly to modern issues of justice, responsibility, and restitution. In today's society, people struggle with issues like property rights, damages, theft, and legal responsibilities. The biblical laws on restitution provide a framework for fairness and personal responsibility. We are reminded of the need to face our own failures and make things right with others, even when it costs us. The idealized self may want to avoid the consequences of wrongdoing, but this passage calls us to face justice with humility and integrity. Whether in personal conflicts, business dealings, or legal matters, this passage reminds us that responsibility and restitution are part of honoring God's justice.

God's Sovereignty and Providence

The laws in this passage reflect God's sovereign care over his people's social and economic lives. By establishing laws of restitution, God shows his providential concern for fairness and order. The laws ensure that everyone is treated justly, and personal losses are restored. God's sovereignty over every aspect of life, including civil matters, challenges the Israelites and us today to trust in his laws as the best guide for justice and well-being. These laws show how God's authority extends into daily life, promoting peace and security for his people. In following these principles, we recognize God's control over societal structures and how they reflect his righteous character.

Covenant Relationship and Faithfulness

The laws of restitution reflect the covenant relationship between God and his people. God calls his people to live in a just and equitable community, where harm and wrongs are addressed fairly. By adhering to these laws, the Israelites demonstrate their faithfulness to the covenant relationship. In the same way, God's faithfulness is reflected in his provision of these laws to protect the vulnerable and ensure justice. In today's context, we are called to live out our covenant obligations by practicing fairness, restitution, and justice in our relationships, workplaces, and communities. Faithfulness to God means being faithful to others by restoring what has been lost and promoting peace.

Human Vocation and Cultural Mandate

The passage aligns with the cultural mandate given in Gen 1:28 to steward and cultivate creation. The laws concerning property, animals, and restitution in Exod 22:1–15 show that part of human vocation is to care for others' goods and to take responsibility when harm is caused. This passage teaches us the value of stewardship—not just of our possessions, but of our relationships and communities. We are called to exercise justice, ensure fairness, and cultivate trust. In the broader cultural context, this might mean working toward laws and policies that promote justice and equity in society.

Common Grace and Resistance to Evil

The laws of restitution reveal God's common grace in providing societal structures that promote justice and order. They help resist evil by ensuring that those who commit theft or damage property are held accountable. By setting up a framework for justice, God's grace restrains evil, promoting peace and fairness. This applies to modern life, where legal systems are designed to resist wrongdoing and promote justice. As Christians, we are called to be part of this resistance by upholding justice, advocating for fair restitution, and living out the principles of justice in our relationships.

God's Grace and Redemptive History

In the broader context of redemptive history, the laws in Exod 22:1–15 reflect God's grace in establishing a just and righteous community. These laws point to the deeper justice and restoration found in Jesus Christ, who paid the ultimate restitution for our sins. Christ's death and resurrection provide the foundation for true justice, where God's wrath is satisfied, and humanity is restored to a right relationship with him. The principles of restitution and justice in Exodus point to the greater redemption found in Christ (Col 1:20), reminding us that God's grace transforms how we live and engage with others in society.

Questions for Reflection and Discussion

1. How does the principle of restitution in Exod 22:1–15 inform our understanding of justice and fairness in today's legal and social systems?

2. In what ways does this passage challenge us to take personal responsibility for the wrongs we have done, and how can we make restitution in our own lives?

3. How does God's concern for justice and fairness in this passage shape our view of his sovereignty and care over all aspects of our lives, including our possessions?

4. How can we apply the principles of stewardship, justice, and restitution in our communities today, whether in business dealings, relationships, or societal issues?

Cultural Mandate and Kingdom Work

In Exod 22:1-15, the cultural mandate of cultivating and stewarding creation is reflected in the laws about property and restitution. The mandate to cultivate and care for creation extends to the social and economic life of the Israelites. These laws encourage responsible stewardship of animals and property (Exod 22:5-6) and fair restitution when harm or theft occurs. When an individual steals livestock or damages someone else's field, they must repay multiple times what they took or harmed (Exod 22:1, 4), reinforcing the idea of nurturing trust and fairness in society. In a modern context, this passage calls us to take responsibility for our work and property, ensure that we restore what we harm, and approach our engagement with the world through a lens of justice and restoration. New Testament connections can be found in passages such as Col 3:23-24, which urges believers to work heartily as for the Lord, reflecting kingdom values in their daily endeavors.

Social Mandate and Family Life

Exodus 22:1-15 underscores the importance of justice and order within the community, which directly impacts social and family dynamics. For example, if a family's livestock is stolen or their field is damaged, it affects their ability to provide for themselves. The restitution laws are in place to protect families from financial ruin and ensure that wrongs are righted fairly. The text teaches that the social structure depends on fair treatment of others' property, promoting the welfare of the community. Godly families and communities are supported by principles of restitution and care, ensuring that no one is unjustly harmed by the wrongdoing of others. The protection of family and property in this passage reflects the larger biblical mandate to care for and protect the family as an institution central to God's purposes (see Eph 6:1-4 for a New Testament view on family life).

Liberty, Justice, and God's Kingdom

This passage reflects God's concern for justice and liberty, as seen in the restitution laws, which balance justice with the liberty of individuals to live in peace. Restitution is not just about punishing the wrongdoer but restoring the freedom and dignity of the person wronged. By requiring restitution to be made multiple times over (Exod 22:1), the passage emphasizes the seriousness of theft and harm, ensuring that the victim's loss is adequately compensated. This emphasis on justice aligns with a broader biblical concern for liberty and righteousness (Isa 61:1), calling God's people to pursue justice that protects individual freedom while maintaining social order. These laws also reflect libertarian ideals grounded in personal responsibility, where individuals are expected to right their wrongs without excessive state interference, allowing for a balanced, righteous pursuit of justice in God's kingdom.

Spiritual Warfare

This section implicitly deals with the spiritual and moral challenges that come with handling wealth and possessions. Property and livestock were vital to the Israelites' livelihoods, and conflicts over these resources could lead to spiritual challenges such as greed, dishonesty, or revenge. The passage calls for integrity in how people deal with one another, ensuring that wrongs are fairly addressed and restitution is made. In terms of spiritual warfare, these laws help protect against the temptation to exploit others for personal gain, as well as the bitterness that could arise from being wronged. As Christians, we are called to reflect God's justice and fairness, resisting the evil of greed or dishonesty (see Eph 6:10-18 for spiritual warfare themes). Standing firm in moral integrity requires that we pursue reconciliation and fairness in our dealings with others, as seen in the principles of restitution and fairness in this chapter.

Questions for Reflection and Discussion

1. How does the principle of restitution in Exod 22:1-15 help us understand God's vision for justice—not merely as punishment but as restoration and repair? In what ways can these principles inform how we handle wrongdoing, loss, or damage in our personal relationships, workplaces, and legal systems today?

2. What does this passage teach us about personal responsibility, especially when harm is caused to others—whether intentionally or accidentally? How can we foster a culture in our families and communities where taking responsibility and making amends is seen as a mark of maturity and faithfulness?

3. How does God's concern for property, fairness, and restitution in this passage shape our view of his sovereignty and care over every aspect of life—including material goods, work, and trust between neighbors? What does this tell us about how we should handle what has been entrusted to us?

4. In what practical ways can Christians today apply the biblical values of stewardship, restitution, and justice to stand against dishonesty, negligence, and exploitation? How can these principles guide us in business, civic engagement, and the building of trust in our communities?

Exodus 22:16—23:9

Context and Analysis

The historical and cultural background of Exod 22:16—23:9 is rooted in Israel's theocratic structure as they prepared to enter the promised land. God was establishing a just society, and these laws were meant to guide the Israelites in their relationships with one another and with God. Key conflicts arise around issues of justice, fairness, and protecting the vulnerable (e.g., women, the poor, foreigners). The characters in this passage—both the offenders and the victims—are part of a broader divine plan for a just society. Repeated themes such as fairness in justice (Exod 23:1-9), protection of the vulnerable (Exod 22:22-23), and the prohibition against oppression (Exod 22:21, 23:9) suggest that control and fear must give way to divine protection and provision. These laws show that God is deeply concerned with both personal holiness and societal justice, highlighting the themes of divine intervention and care for the marginalized.

Spiritual Insights: Basic Anxiety

The anxieties in this passage often stem from the fear of oppression and injustice, particularly for the vulnerable. For example, women who are seduced (Exod 22:16) or foreigners who are oppressed (Exod 22:21) may feel helpless. Some might cope by seeking dominance, like those who take advantage of the poor, or by self-effacing submission, as the vulnerable often do. The passage warns against trusting in human strength or systems of oppression and calls instead for trusting in God's justice and provision (Exod 22:23-24). Their actions—whether oppressors or victims—are shaped by either reliance on self or faith in God. When the Israelites fail to trust in

God's provision and take matters into their own hands, they become complicit in injustice, which breaks their relationship with God.

Problems and Dilemmas

The moral and spiritual dilemmas in this passage revolve around the conflict between pursuing personal gain versus upholding justice. For instance, the issue of seduction (Exod 22:16–17) highlights a dilemma between individual desires and the integrity of family and community. Similarly, the call for honesty in legal disputes (Exod 23:1–3) forces the Israelites to choose between truth and falsehood. The real self—marked by human struggles like greed, lust, and power—stands in contrast to the ideal self, which God calls them to embody through obedience and righteousness. The text challenges readers to reflect on their motivations for obedience: are they acting out of fear, control, or true faithfulness to God's commands?

Themes and Obligations

The overarching theme in Exod 22:16—23:9 is God's protection versus human vulnerability. God's laws are meant to protect the weak and vulnerable, like women, the poor, and foreigners (Exod 22:21–25). The characters' responses highlight whether they trust in divine provision or rely on their own strength. Those who care for the vulnerable demonstrate trust in God, while those who oppress or manipulate others reveal a reliance on their own power. The ethical responsibilities of this text are clear: do not oppress or harm others, especially the vulnerable, and be just in all your dealings. This passage challenges readers to act with nobility, fairness, and integrity, even when tempted by self-interest or fear.

Reflections and Application

This passage speaks powerfully to modern struggles with insecurity and anxiety, especially regarding justice and fairness in relationships and society. It challenges readers to think about how they treat others, particularly those in vulnerable positions. The concept of the idealized self—the unrealistic drive for perfection—may manifest in legalistic or self-righteous behavior, where one follows the letter of the law while ignoring its spirit. The laws in Exodus call for a higher form of justice that reflects God's character. In modern contexts of leadership, community challenges, and personal struggles with identity and purpose, these laws remind us to prioritize justice, truth, and compassion over selfish ambition.

God's Sovereignty and Providence

God's sovereignty is evident in his establishment of laws that promote justice and protect the vulnerable. The laws in Exod 22:16—23:9 reveal God's control over all aspects of life, from interpersonal relationships to the judicial system. His providence is displayed in his care for the vulnerable and his demand for fairness in all areas of life. This passage calls us to submit to God's authority, trusting that his laws are designed for the well-being of all people. It challenges us to recognize God's sovereignty not just in spiritual matters but in societal and personal leadership as well (Rom 13:1–4).

Covenant Relationship and Faithfulness

This section reflects the covenant relationship between God and his people, emphasizing the responsibilities that come with being part of God's chosen community. The laws serve as a reminder that faithfulness to God is reflected in how his people treat one another, especially the vulnerable (Exod 22:21–23). God's faithfulness to his covenant promises is seen in his protection and provision for the weak and oppressed. As Christians, we are called to live out our covenant obligations by being faithful to God's commands and reflecting his justice and mercy in our communities (Heb 8:10).

Human Vocation and Cultural Mandate

The human vocation, according to Exod 22:16—23:9, includes the responsibility to uphold justice, fairness, and compassion in society. This passage highlights the stewardship God's people are called to exercise over relationships and resources. By protecting the vulnerable, upholding the truth, and ensuring fairness, God's people fulfill their cultural mandate to steward and develop creation in a way that reflects God's justice and love. The call to work and serve in a way that cultivates the world for God's kingdom is made clear through the laws of justice and restitution (Exod 22:5–6). This extends to modern work environments, community involvement, and family life, where Christians are called to cultivate justice and mercy (Mic 6:8).

Common Grace and Resistance to Evil

This section portrays the tension between good and evil through the laws that resist injustice, exploitation, and oppression. God's grace operates to sustain a society where fairness and righteousness are upheld, even in a fallen world. The laws in Exod 22:16—23:9 are an expression of common grace, ensuring the well-being of all people, not just the Israelites. These laws challenge us to resist evil by protecting the vulnerable, upholding justice, and rejecting corruption. In modern life, this may involve resisting systems of oppression, standing up for the marginalized, and ensuring that truth prevails in our communities and institutions (Rom 12:9).

God's Grace and Redemptive History

This section demonstrates God's grace in redemptive history by outlining laws that aim to restore relationships and promote justice. These laws reflect God's desire for his people to live in harmony with one another and with him. The principles of justice and restitution (Exod 22:1–4) are part of God's redemptive work, pointing forward to Christ's ultimate sacrifice, which brings reconciliation between God and humanity (Col 1:19–20). As Christians, we are called to participate in God's mission of restoring all things, applying these principles of justice, mercy, and grace in our interactions with others.

Cultural Mandate and Kingdom Work

In Exod 22:16—23:9, the cultural mandate is demonstrated in the protection and care for others' rights and property, as well as justice and fairness in community life. The laws here concerning personal conduct (e.g., treatment of women, foreigners, the poor, and workers in Exod 22:22–23 and 23:4–6) remind us of God's command to steward not only the land but also our relationships and societal systems. This passage calls us to uphold justice, seek the welfare of the vulnerable, and cultivate an environment where fairness and responsibility thrive. For contemporary application, Christians are called to advocate for justice in their work and social interactions, ensuring that all people are treated with dignity and fairness, aligning with Christ's teachings on loving others (Matt 22:39).

Social Mandate and Family Life

Exodus 22:16—23:9 emphasizes the social dynamics of God's people, particularly the responsibilities toward vulnerable groups like widows, orphans, and the poor (Exod 22:22-25). The care and protection of these groups reflect a broader responsibility to uphold God's order in family and community life. The protection of young women in cases of seduction (Exod 22:16-17) also points to the importance of guarding family honor and respecting relational integrity. Families and communities thrive when they operate within God's ordained structure, ensuring justice, mercy, and compassion. In a modern context, this passage reminds us of our obligation to create strong, godly families and communities where all members, especially the vulnerable, are supported (Jas 1:27).

Liberty, Justice, and God's Kingdom

This passage reflects God's concern for justice and liberty through laws that establish fairness and protect the vulnerable from oppression (Exod 22:21; 23:6-9). The commands to not oppress foreigners (Exod 22:21) and to provide justice for the poor (Exod 23:6) emphasize God's desire for a society where political and economic liberty align with divine righteousness. These verses call God's people to be defenders of justice, ensuring that liberty is upheld for everyone, especially for those who are powerless. From a libertarian perspective, these laws guard individual rights and protect freedom from excessive or abusive authority. Christians today are called to engage in justice that reflects the kingdom of God, where righteousness and fairness reign (Isa 61:1-3).

Spiritual Warfare

Exodus 22:16—23:9 deals with moral and spiritual integrity in daily life. God commands his people to live justly and uphold moral integrity in matters of personal conduct, treatment of others, and judicial fairness (Exod 23:1-9). The instructions to avoid false testimony, resist bribes, and uphold truth (Exod 23:1, 8) highlight the moral challenges God's people face in a fallen world. These verses encourage God's people to pursue righteousness and to stand firm against the temptation to manipulate justice or harm others for personal gain. In terms of spiritual warfare, these commands equip believers to resist evil by embodying justice, truth, and mercy in their lives, much like Paul's exhortation in Eph 6:10-18 to wear the full armor of God.

Questions for Reflection and Discussion

1. How does the vision of justice in Exod 22:16—23:9—especially in areas like restitution, sexual ethics, fair treatment of foreigners, and impartiality—challenge our understanding of what a just and holy society looks like? How can we begin applying these principles in our personal conduct, workplaces, and civic responsibilities?

2. In this passage, God repeatedly emphasizes care for the vulnerable—such as widows, orphans, the poor, and sojourners. How can we, as individuals and as a church, more intentionally structure our lives and ministries to reflect God's heart for those who are often overlooked, excluded, or exploited?

3. What does this passage teach us about God's character as both just and merciful? How should this dual emphasis shape the way we approach difficult situations involving conflict, reconciliation, or advocacy—whether in our homes, workplaces, or broader communities?

4. In a culture that often rewards compromise, favoritism, and the pursuit of self-interest, how does this passage call us to moral courage and integrity? What are some specific ways we can resist evil, uphold truth, and engage in spiritual warfare through just and faithful living today?

Exodus 23:10-31

Context and Analysis

Exodus 23:10-31 addresses God's commandments regarding sabbatical years, festivals, and the promise of his presence as Israel enters the promised land. This period in Israel's history is post-exodus, and the nation is being formed under God's law, distinct from neighboring nations. The instructions set Israel apart as a holy nation, highlighting their dependence on God for sustenance, rest, and worship. The Israelites face a variety of challenges, including learning how to trust God's provision during the fallow year, as well as understanding how to practice justice and hospitality within their social and agricultural practices. They are also called to maintain covenant faithfulness amidst threats from other nations. The Israelites are asked to trust God's power in both provision (through the sabbatical year) and protection (God's promise to send an angel before them, v. 20). They must practice vulnerability by relying on God for protection against external threats. Key characters such as Moses, representing Israel's leadership, and God, who promises to drive out the enemies, engage in a divine-human relationship where trust in God's sovereignty is central. Themes of rest and protection repeat in this passage. The sabbatical year (Exod 23:11) symbolizes rest and reliance on God's provision, while the promise of God's angel (Exod 23:20) symbolizes divine protection and guidance.

Spiritual Insights: Basic Anxiety

The Israelites are asked to leave their land uncultivated every seventh year, a command that could provoke anxiety about provision. Additionally, as they prepare to confront their enemies, fear over their ability to inhabit the promised land might emerge. In response to anxiety, the Israelites could choose to trust God (faith-based response) or rely on their own efforts. The command to follow God's angel without rebellion (Exod 23:21) implies that their success is contingent on obedience to God rather than self-reliance. Trusting in God's provision during the sabbatical year (Exod 23:11) and in his protection (Exod 23:22) deepens the covenant relationship. Failure to trust would result in their spiritual and physical vulnerability. This teaches that reliance on self leads to insecurity, whereas trusting in God brings peace and provision (Phil 4:6–7).

Problems and Dilemmas

One dilemma revolves around the tension between resting (through sabbatical laws) and working to ensure provision. This challenges the Israelites to balance diligence with dependence on God. Another dilemma is the temptation to conform to pagan practices, as God warns them not to make covenants with other nations or serve their gods (Exod 23:24, 32). The Israelites' struggle highlights the battle between controlling outcomes through human means versus exercising faith in God's commands. The dilemma of making alliances with foreign nations (Exod 23:32) also underscores fear of vulnerability and the desire for security. The real self struggles with fear and uncertainty over provision, while the idealized self is called to unwavering trust in God's promises. The call to obedience in following God's angel (Exod 23:20) points to the reality of human weakness contrasted with the ideal of perfect faith.

Themes and Obligations

God promises to protect Israel from its enemies and to drive them out little by little (Exod 23:30). The Israelites' vulnerability is addressed through divine intervention, but they are tasked with remaining faithful, not making alliances with pagan nations, and refraining from idolatry (Exod 23:24). This passage emphasizes reliance on God for both physical (sabbatical provision) and spiritual (deliverance from enemies) needs. The Israelites are morally obligated to uphold God's law, including honoring the sabbatical and keeping the festivals (Exod 23:14–17).

Reflections and Application

Like the Israelites, modern believers often wrestle with trusting God's provision, whether in financial security or divine protection. This passage reminds us that God's faithfulness in the past should encourage us to trust him in present uncertainties. The unrealistic drive for self-sufficiency contrasts with the biblical call to rest in God's provision and timing. The passage offers encouragement to surrender control, especially in seasons of rest and trust (such as during sabbaticals or rest periods in our own lives). In modern times, as people navigate leadership and community challenges, this passage encourages reliance on God's guidance rather than human strength. In leadership roles, this means trusting God's sovereignty in decisions and outcomes, and in personal struggles, it means embracing seasons of rest and faith in God's provision.

God's Sovereignty and Providence

The sabbatical laws (Exod 23:10–11) reflect God's sovereignty over creation, reminding Israel that the land belongs to him and he provides even when it lies fallow. This challenges modern readers to acknowledge God's ownership over all things and to trust his providence in every area of life (Matt 6:26). God's promise to lead Israel through his angel (Exod 23:20) shows his authority over nations and their destiny. This underscores the biblical truth that leaders are to follow God's direction faithfully, recognizing that ultimate success comes from divine rather than human efforts.

Covenant Relationship and Faithfulness

The covenant relationship requires Israel's obedience and faithfulness. God's promise to drive out their enemies (Exod 23:22–23) is contingent on their fidelity. This reflects the broader covenantal theme of conditional blessings and curses, where obedience brings life, and rebellion brings death. Modern believers are called to live out their covenant obligations through obedience and faithfulness to Christ. This involves trusting God's provision, resisting cultural idols, and living out biblical principles in all spheres of life.

Stewardship and Creation Care

The command for sabbatical rest (Exod 23:11) teaches stewardship of creation. By resting the land, Israel is fulfilling the cultural mandate to care for and develop the earth responsibly (Gen 1:28). Today, this translates into responsible environmental stewardship and sustainable practices in our work and communities. The festivals (Exod 23:14–17) and sabbatical laws remind believers of the rhythm of work and rest, showing that both are essential in participating in God's mission of restoration. Christians are called to engage in their work as a form of kingdom service while also embracing the biblical command to rest.

Common Grace and Resistance to Evil

The command to avoid covenants with pagan nations (Exod 23:32) and to resist idolatry highlights the spiritual battle between good and evil. This is mirrored in the New Testament where Christians are called to resist evil influences and keep themselves unstained from the world (Jas 1:27). God's grace is evident in his promise to protect Israel from external threats while calling them to uphold justice and righteousness internally. In the modern world, believers are tasked with resisting cultural evils while relying on God's grace to sustain them in the fight.

God's Grace and Redemptive History

The promise of God's angel guiding Israel (Exod 23:20) is a foreshadowing of Christ as the ultimate guide and protector of his people. God's grace throughout history, from Israel's deliverance to Christ's sacrifice, underscores his plan of redemption that continues today. As agents of redemption, Christians are called to apply God's grace in their involvement with societal issues, striving for justice and mercy as part of their participation in God's ongoing work of restoration.

Cultural Mandate and Kingdom Work

In Exod 23:10–31, the cultural mandate is clearly seen in the command to observe the sabbatical year: "For six years you are to sow your fields and harvest the crops, but during the seventh year let the land lie unplowed and unused" (Exod 23:10–11). This practice highlights the biblical principle of stewardship over creation, reminding Israel that the land belongs to God and that they are caretakers of his creation. This aligns with the original cultural mandate given in Gen 1:28, where humanity is called to cultivate and care for the earth. By allowing the land to rest, they were also to provide for the poor and wild animals, which reflects the care for others that is central to kingdom work.

Application Today: In modern contexts, this principle calls Christians to balance work and rest, honoring the created order through sustainable practices. We are called to steward resources well and prioritize renewal, both environmentally and in personal rhythms of work and rest, participating in God's mission to restore all things (Col 1:20).

Social Mandate and Family Life

This section also addresses family and social dynamics by emphasizing justice and care for the vulnerable. The sabbatical year and the festivals (Exod 23:14–17) create opportunities for families and communities to gather and celebrate God's provision together. The focus on leaving some of the harvest for the poor and wild animals (Exod 23:11) reinforces the call to uphold social responsibility and to ensure that even the marginalized in society are provided for. This passage highlights the idea of a community that looks after its weakest members and honors God's design for family and community structures.

Application Today: God's people today are called to uphold family life and social order by providing for those in need, caring for vulnerable communities, and practicing hospitality. Healthy family and community life is central to advancing God's purposes in the world (1 Tim 5:8).

Liberty, Justice, and God's Kingdom

Exodus 23:10–31 reveals God's concern for justice, especially in how Israel is commanded to avoid oppression and idolatry (Exod 23:13, 24). The call to justice is also seen in the treatment of others during the sabbatical year. Additionally, the command to not oppress foreigners (Exod 23:9) shows God's concern for economic and political liberty. God's promises of victory and territorial expansion (Exod 23:27–31) emphasize liberty under God's rule, where his people would live free from oppression and secure in his protection.

Application Today: Christians are called to pursue justice in ways that promote liberty for all people, grounded in God's righteousness. The biblical principle of not oppressing others extends to advocating for justice in political, economic, and social systems today, in a manner that reflects the coming kingdom of God (Mic 6:8).

Spiritual Warfare

This passage deals with the moral and spiritual challenges Israel would face as they entered the promised land. God promises to drive out their enemies (Exod 23:27–31) but warns them not to make covenants with the nations or worship their gods (Exod 23:32–33). The struggle between serving God and succumbing to idolatry highlights the spiritual battle that the Israelites would face. God's command to destroy the idols of the nations (Exod 23:24) reinforces the need for moral integrity and spiritual vigilance.

Application Today: Believers today are engaged in spiritual warfare, standing firm against the temptations and moral challenges of the world. Christians must remain vigilant, avoiding the idolatry of materialism, power, or self-reliance, while living with integrity and trusting in God's protection and provision (Eph 6:12–13).

Questions for Reflection and Discussion

1. How does the command for a sabbatical year challenge our assumptions about productivity, ownership, and provision? In what practical ways can we cultivate rhythms of rest, generosity, and trust in God's care within our families, workplaces, and communities?

2. In Exod 23, God commands his people to show justice and mercy to the poor, to rest the land, and to reject falsehood and oppression. How can we practice this kind of justice and compassion in a world driven by efficiency, wealth accumulation, and power dynamics?

3. God promises to guide, protect, and bless his people if they remain faithful, while warning them against making covenants with the nations and idols around them. What modern forms of compromise or idolatry threaten our allegiance to God today, and how can we resist them with spiritual integrity?

4. This passage highlights God's gradual, intentional leadership in bringing Israel into the promised land. How does this encourage us to trust God's timing in our pursuit of justice, growth, and renewal in our lives and society? What are ways we can actively follow his lead rather than rushing ahead in our own strength?

Exodus 24

Context and Analysis

Exodus 24 represents a key moment in the covenant relationship between God and Israel. The historical background is the ratification of the Mosaic covenant after God has delivered the Ten Commandments and the laws that follow. The covenant ceremony involves blood sacrifices, the reading of the law, and a meal shared in God's presence (Exod 24:3–11). Moses, Aaron, Nadab, Abihu, and seventy elders of Israel ascend Mount Sinai. The repeated theme of the mountain as the meeting place between God and man emphasizes divine transcendence, while the use of blood in the covenant points to atonement and the seriousness of Israel's commitment. Symbols like the blood of the covenant (Exod 24:6–8) and the tablets of the law (Exod 24:12) emphasize God's holiness, justice, and desire for obedience. The mountain's trembling and the cloud signify divine intervention and awe-inspiring control.

Spiritual Insights: Basic Anxiety

The characters experience fear and vulnerability throughout the passage. Israel's fear is palpable when they are asked to obey everything the LORD has said (Exod 24:3). The symbolism of the blood sprinkled on the people underscores their awareness of sin and the need for atonement. The elders, who behold God, do so with both reverence and fear (Exod 24:10). The Israelites demonstrate trust in God, as opposed to self-reliance, by submitting to the covenant. Trusting in the self would have led to insecurity, but trusting in God's provision through the covenant promises brings peace, even amidst fear.

Problems and Dilemmas

A dilemma in this passage is the Israelites' struggle between obeying God's law and the temptation to disobey. The covenant commitment requires total obedience, as expressed by the people's declaration, "We will do everything the LORD has said" (Exod 24:3). This poses a dilemma because human frailty means they will struggle to meet God's perfect standards. The contrast between their real selves—frail and sinful—and the idealized expectation of perfection is highlighted. The issue of leadership also surfaces, as Moses ascends the mountain to receive the law, leaving the people to await his return.

Themes and Obligations

This passage emphasizes God's protection and human vulnerability. The people of Israel, who rely on God's protection, are reminded of their obligation to uphold their part of the covenant by obeying his law. The use of blood symbolizes atonement, and the meal shared with God signifies fellowship and reconciliation (Exod 24:11). The ethical responsibility to be faithful to the covenant challenges the people to think about duty and justice. Moses models nobility of character by leading the people faithfully in response to God's commands, while the elders demonstrate humility in their encounter with God.

Reflections and Application

This passage speaks to modern struggles with obedience and fear of failure. The Israelites' declaration to do everything the LORD has commanded might resonate with those who feel pressured to meet unattainable expectations. The lesson is that while perfection is not attainable, God's grace and the covenantal relationship he provides offer security and hope. This can be applied to leadership, where trust in God's provision is crucial in the face of challenges. Today, leaders and communities might draw from this passage in their struggles with moral integrity and communal responsibility.

God's Sovereignty and Providence

Exodus 24 reveals God's absolute sovereignty in establishing his covenant with Israel. God is the one who initiates the covenant, provides the law, and ensures the means of atonement through the sacrificial blood (Exod

24:8). The people's response of obedience underscores their recognition of God's authority over their lives. This passage challenges believers to trust in God's sovereignty and providence in every area of life, whether in personal struggles or societal leadership. God's control is seen in his guidance of Israel through Moses.

Covenant Relationship and Faithfulness

The passage emphasizes the covenant relationship between God and his people. The blood of the covenant (Exod 24:8) signifies the sealing of this relationship, binding the people of Israel to their commitments. The faithfulness of God, who provides both the law and the sacrificial system, encourages Israel to respond with loyalty and obedience. This theme translates into modern life, where Christians are called to live out their covenant obligations by being faithful to God, his church, and their communities (Heb 9:15).

Human Vocation and Cultural Mandate

This section highlights the call to obedience as part of the Israelites' vocation. God gives his law to be lived out as an expression of his kingdom principles on earth. Stewardship is seen in the people's responsibility to uphold justice, righteousness, and God's moral order. Today, believers are called to exercise similar stewardship by cultivating justice, serving others, and reflecting God's kingdom in their work and rest.

Common Grace and Resistance to Evil

The tension between good and evil is present in the Israelites' obligation to uphold the covenant in a sinful world. God's grace, symbolized by the blood of the covenant, operates to preserve his people and sustain their commitment to him. Despite their vulnerability to sin and failure, God's grace provides the means to remain faithful. Christians today are similarly called to resist evil, recognizing that God's grace is active in their lives, empowering them to persevere in faith.

God's Grace and Redemptive History

This section reflects God's grace in redemptive history through the covenant relationship he establishes. The sprinkling of blood points forward to the ultimate sacrifice of Christ, who mediates a new covenant (Heb 9:15). God's grace in this covenant transforms how his people live, not only within the church but also in their engagement with the world. This redemptive work of God informs believers' involvement in societal and cultural issues today, shaping their approach to justice, community, and leadership.

Cultural Mandate and Kingdom Work

In Exod 24, the cultural mandate is seen in God's act of formalizing the covenant with his people, calling them to live in obedience to his law. The mandate to cultivate and steward creation expands to include the work of faithfully living out God's commands. In verse 12, God tells Moses to come up the mountain to receive the law and commandments written on stone tablets, which would guide Israel's life. This reflects the call to steward the world not just materially, but spiritually, by aligning their lives with God's righteous order. In today's context, this mandate encourages us to engage in both work and rest as acts of worship, participating in God's mission to restore creation. Colossians 3:23–24 reminds us to work as unto the Lord, viewing all aspects of life as avenues for kingdom renewal.

Social Mandate and Family Life

Exodus 24 highlights the importance of communal and familial obedience to God's commands. The entire assembly of Israel is involved in affirming the covenant (Exod 24:3–8). The repeated declaration, "We will do everything the Lord has said," shows the collective commitment to upholding God's order within their society, including family structures. The family, as a building block of Israel's society, would play a key role in passing on the covenant promises and law to future generations. This section teaches us the importance of strong, godly families and communities that adhere to God's purposes. Ephesians 6:4 echoes this by urging parents to bring up their children in the instruction of the Lord, emphasizing the role of families in shaping covenant faithfulness.

Liberty, Justice, and God's Kingdom

The covenant ceremony in Exod 24 points to God's concern for justice and liberty, as his laws are given to protect and govern his people in righteousness. The sprinkling of blood on the people and the altar (Exod 24:6–8) symbolizes both the seriousness of the covenant and the provision for justice through atonement. God's law is a foundation for political and social justice, ensuring liberty from oppression and maintaining order in society. The chapter encourages believers today to pursue justice and liberty grounded in God's righteousness, reflecting the values of the coming kingdom of God. Galatians 5:1 speaks to this liberty, stating that Christ has set us free, calling us to live in that freedom while adhering to God's righteous standards.

Spiritual Warfare

Exodus 24 emphasizes the spiritual and moral challenges faced by Israel. The covenant required the people to trust God's law and maintain integrity in their obedience. The passage shows the struggle between moral failure and God's provision for atonement through the sacrificial system. The elders who ascend the mountain and eat with God (Exod 24:9–11) represent the tension between humanity's sinfulness and the holiness required to enter God's presence. For us today, this chapter teaches that life is a battleground where spiritual warfare is real, and moral integrity is essential. Ephesians 6:12 reminds us that we wrestle not against flesh and blood, but against spiritual forces of evil, highlighting the need to stand firm in faith.

Questions for Reflection and Discussion

1. What does the covenant ceremony in Exod 24 teach us about the seriousness of our commitment to God? How can the imagery of blood, law, and shared fellowship shape our understanding of obedience today—not as legalism, but as a response to grace and a way of living faithfully in community?

2. In what ways do we struggle with the same tension Israel faced between their promises of obedience and the reality of human frailty? How can God's grace, seen in both the sacrificial system and ultimately in Christ, reshape how we deal with failure, leadership responsibility, and spiritual growth?

3. How does the image of the elders beholding God and eating in his presence (Exod 24:9–11) challenge our understanding of what it means to approach God in reverence and relationship? What can this teach us about worship, leadership, and intimacy with God in both private and corporate life?

4. In a world where integrity, justice, and truth are often compromised, how does the covenant in Exod 24 equip us to resist moral drift and spiritual apathy? What practical steps can we take—as individuals and as communities—to remain faithful to God's law while living out the hope and renewal of his kingdom in daily life?

Conclusion

Our journey through the initial, formative chapters of Exodus has been an exploration of God's mighty hand at work—rescuing his people from the crucible of oppression, revealing his character in power and holiness, and establishing a covenant that would define their identity and mission. We have walked with Israel from the bitterness of slavery to the awe-inspiring encounter at Sinai, witnessing firsthand how God's commitment to his promises unfolds in tangible, history-shaping ways. Through the lens of loving God and neighbor, and with the insightful frameworks of thinkers like Van Groningen, Kuyper, Horney, and Niebuhr, we hope you have gained a richer understanding of God's redemptive purposes and the profound complexities of the human condition in response to divine initiative.

You have seen God's sovereign kingdom advance against the empires of this world (Kuyper, Van Groningen), and the deep anxieties and coping mechanisms that surface in both oppressors and the oppressed when faced with divine power and human vulnerability (Horney, Niebuhr). This multifaceted approach—examining the theological currents, the psychological depths, and the societal implications—is not merely an academic exercise. It is a pathway to a more integrated faith, one that sees God at work in every sphere of life and calls us to respond with our whole beings.

But the story of God's work and humanity's response does not conclude with the ratification of the covenant at Sinai. The book of Exodus, powerful as it is, forms the heart of a larger, foundational narrative: the Pentateuch. The same depth of engagement, the same willingness to explore the interplay of divine action and human experience, and the same commitment to applying these truths to our personal lives, our churches, and our society, will yield even greater treasures as you continue your journey through the remaining books of Moses.

I fervently encourage you to carry this approach forward. First, return to Genesis, the book of origins. Here, the covenantal, kingdom, and mediatorial themes (Van Groningen) are established from creation itself. Witness the goodness of God's design for human flourishing within distinct spheres (Kuyper), the entry of sin born from anxiety and the desire for autonomy (Niebuhr), and the subsequent patterns of human striving and relational brokenness (Horney) that set the stage for God's redemptive plan. See how God's promises to the patriarchs lay the very groundwork for the deliverance you have just studied in Exodus.

Then, venture into Leviticus. Far from being a dry legal code, Leviticus, when read with an eye for God's character and our human condition, reveals the profound provisions God makes for a sinful people to dwell in the presence of a holy God. Explore how its rituals and laws address human anxieties about guilt and defilement (Horney, Niebuhr), establish order and justice within the covenant community (Kuyper), and point forward to the ultimate mediator and sacrifice (Van Groningen). Understanding Leviticus is key to grasping the depth of God's holiness and the seriousness of his call to his people to reflect that holiness in every sphere.

Next, navigate the complexities of Numbers. This book chronicles Israel's wilderness wanderings, a period marked by profound human failure, rebellion, and the anxieties of a people struggling to trust God's provision (Horney, Niebuhr). Yet, amidst the grumbling and judgment, God's covenant faithfulness (Van Groningen) and sovereign guidance (Kuyper) shine through. Numbers is a stark reminder of the consequences of unbelief but also a testament to God's enduring patience and his commitment to bringing his people into their inheritance.

Finally, immerse yourself in Deuteronomy. Here, Moses delivers his farewell addresses, passionately rearticulating the covenant for a new generation about to enter the promised land. It is a call to heartfelt obedience, rooted in the remembrance of God's mighty acts (a theme central to Exodus) and a vision for a society where every sphere of life is ordered under God's loving and just rule (Kuyper). Deuteronomy powerfully connects right worship with right living, urging Israel to love God and neighbor as the foundation of their national life.

The God who was so powerfully at work in Exodus continues his work throughout the Pentateuch, laying the foundations for all that follows in Scripture and culminating in the person and work of Jesus Christ. By applying the rich, layered reading you have practiced here, you will uncover deeper connections, gain profounder insights into God's character, and be better equipped to live as his faithful people in a complex world. May your study be a continual encounter with the living God, transforming your heart, mind, and actions for his glory and the good of your neighbor.

Bibliography

Bratt, James D., ed. *Abraham Kuyper: A Centennial Reader*. Grand Rapids: Eerdmans, 1998.

Christian Reformed Church. Heidelberg Catechism. https://www.crcna.org/welcome/beliefs/confessions/heidelberg-catechism.

Henry, Matthew. *Matthew Henry's Commentary on the Whole Bible*. Accessed June 30, 2025. https://www.blueletterbible.org/commentaries/henry_matthew/.

Horney, Karen. *Neurosis and Human Growth: The Struggle Toward Self-Realization*. New York: Norton, 1950.

Niebuhr, Reinhold. *Moral Man and Immoral Society: A Study in Ethics and Politics*. Louisville: Westminster John Knox, 2021.

———. *The Nature and Destiny of Man: A Christian Interpretation*. 2 vols. Martino Fine Books, 2018.

Tuininga, Matthew J. "Abraham Kuyper and the Social Order: Principles for Christian Liberalism." *Journal of Markets & Morality* 23 (2020) 337–61.

Van Groningen, Gerard. *From Creation to Consummation: A Biblical Theology of the Kingdom of God*. Vol. 1. Sioux Center, IA: Dordt College Press, 1996.

www.ingramcontent.com/pod-product-compliance
Lightning Source LLC
Chambersburg PA
CBHW072127160426
43197CB00012B/2026